# USING CLASSIC WAL[K

G000271689

**DISTANCE**
# 5
**MILES**

**DISTANCE:**
Rounded to the nearest half mile.

**REFRESHMENTS & TOILETS**

facilities, bear in mind tha[
(Oct. to Easter).

**WALK GRADE:**
● **EASY:** Well within the reach of most families and largely on level terrain.
● **MODERATE:** Requiring more exertion and likely to include some sections of uphill walking.
● **TOUGH:** More strenuous routes involving sections of steep climb and/or rough terrain.

**TIME**
# 3.5
**HOURS**

**TIME:**
Rounded to the nearest half hour.

*WALK MODERATE GRADE*

As with all walks books, *Classic Walks: Cornwall 2* will stay in pristine condition if you avoid getting the book wet. *Classic Walks: Cornwall 2* has been designed to fit into most map holders; a cheap and effective alternative is to use one of the supermarkets' produce bags which are thin enough to allow you to read your walk directions!

If you prefer to have an Ordnance Survey map with you, the new orange 1: 25 000 Explorer maps are good value for money and very detailed.

**MAP REF.**
ORDNANCE SURVEY LANDRANGER 200
# 915
754

**MAP REF.:**
Refers to the start point car park.

**N.B.** It is advisable to ALWAYS assume that parts of any route could be muddy or wet under foot. Walking shoes or boots are strongly advised.

# YOUR WALKS RECORD

Use this to record the dates on which you completed each walk:

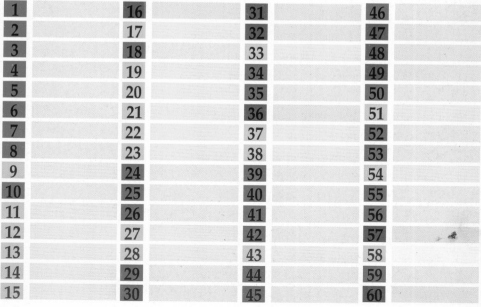

| 1 | | 16 | | 31 | | 46 | |
| 2 | | 17 | | 32 | | 47 | |
| 3 | | 18 | | 33 | | 48 | |
| 4 | | 19 | | 34 | | 49 | |
| 5 | | 20 | | 35 | | 50 | |
| 6 | | 21 | | 36 | | 51 | |
| 7 | | 22 | | 37 | | 52 | |
| 8 | | 23 | | 38 | | 53 | |
| 9 | | 24 | | 39 | | 54 | |
| 10 | | 25 | | 40 | | 55 | |
| 11 | | 26 | | 41 | | 56 | |
| 12 | | 27 | | 42 | | 57 | |
| 13 | | 28 | | 43 | | 58 | |
| 14 | | 29 | | 44 | | 59 | |
| 15 | | 30 | | 45 | | 60 | |

1

# CLASSIC WALKS: CONTENTS

The 60 walks in this book have been divided into these three grades:

 WALK EASY GRADE

 WALK MODERATE GRADE

 WALK TOUGH GRADE

# CLASSIC WALKS CORNWALL 2

## WALK GRADE

■ EASY: Well within the reach of most families and largely on level terrain.

■ MODERATE: Requiring more exertion and likely to include some sections of uphill walking.

■ TOUGH: More strenuous routes involving sections of steep climb and/or rough terrain.

N.B. This map, like the maps for the walks, is not to scale and for diagramatic purposes only.

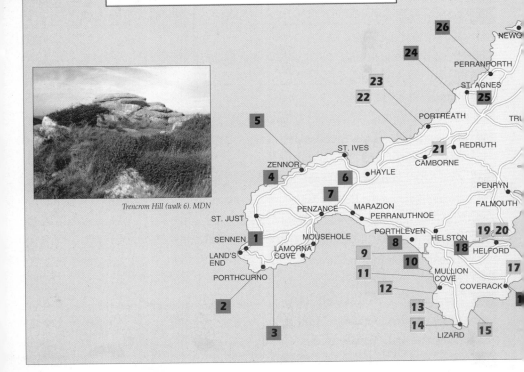

*Trencrom Hill (walk 6). MDN*

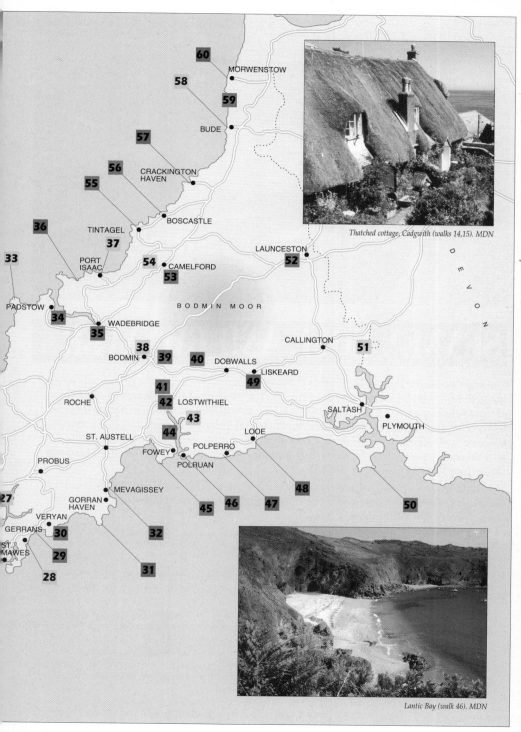

60
MORWENSTOW
58
59
BUDE
57
CRACKINGTON
HAVEN
56
55
BOSCASTLE
36
TINTAGEL
37
33
PORT
ISAAC
54
CAMELFORD
53
LAUNCESTON
52
PADSTOW

D E V O N

34
WADEBRIDGE
35
BODMIN MOOR
38
BODMIN
39
40
DOBWALLS
CALLINGTON
51
ROCHE
41
42
LOSTWITHIEL
LISKEARD
49
ST. AUSTELL
43
44
LOOE
SALTASH
FOWEY
POLPERRO
PLYMOUTH
PROBUS
POLRUAN
27
MEVAGISSEY
48
GORRAN
HAVEN
45
46
47
VERYAN
50
GERRANS
30
32
ST.
MAWES
29
31
28

*Thatched cottage, Cadgwith (walks 14,15). MDN*

*Lantic Bay (walk 46). MDN*

*Sennen Cove. MDN*

# SENNEN COVE AND GWYNVER

*The start point for this walk, Sennen Cove, is the most westerly village in England and blessed with one of Cornwall's best beaches. The gloriously white sands of the bay attract families whilst westerly winds provide conditions suitable for the surfing fraternity. Across the bay can be seen the National Trust owned headland of Cape Cornwall; the distinctive chimney a relic from its mining past. There are several refreshment opportunities in the village and an early evening visit, providing views of the setting sun can be a sheer delight.*

*The walk route initially follows the coastpath around Whitesand Bay to the beach at Gwynver (pronounced Gwen-ver). An inland track leading to field paths and narrow lanes provide the return on this circular walk.*

| | |
|---|---|
| **REFRESHMENTS & TOILETS** | At Sennen Cove (start point). |
| **DIRECTIONS TO START** | Follow the A30 towards Land's End before taking the turning for Sennen Cove. Use the large car park at the bottom on the right. |

## WALK DIRECTIONS

From a position of looking out to sea, bear right to find the coastpath marked up steps in the far corner of the car park. Follow the coastpath, keeping the sands of Whitesand Bay below left. The headland of Cape Cornwall, with its distinctive chimney, can be seen in the distance. As the path starts to approach some cottages in a narrow valley, bear left on a sandy path descending towards the beach. Cross a stream at the bottom and then bear right to find a fenced path through the dunes, next to a yellow triangle indicating a telephone cable. After a few yards, bear left, following a fence to reach a concrete bunker. From here, follow a more definite coastal path. After a while, the granite studded coastpath descends to pass behind the attractive beach at Gwynver.

Walk to the rear of the beach, continuing ahead before passing over a small stile in a stone boundary that leads up the hill on the right. A few yards after this stile, leave the coastpath and bear right on a faint path that leads uphill through the gorse. Where the path emerges into a field, proceed ahead, diagonally half left, towards two gates in walls. Pass through the top gate and follow a narrow, fairly overgrown track, between hedges.

The track passes through a gate before continuing through a metal gate to use a lane that proceeds between farm buildings. Walk away from the farm, descending. At the bottom of the lane, just before it bears off left, notice a gate and pathway sign on the right. Cross the stile here and walk on a slightly right bearing across the field to cross a further stile and field. Reach and cross a third stile and walk across a

large field towards a line of telegraph poles. The track now follows the telegraph poles before passing through a gate to reach a tarmac lane.

Follow the lane, passing a house called Peace and Plenty. Where the road bears to the left, bear sharp right on an unmade lane, a thatched cottage off to the left. This lane leads onto an earth track, Gwynver Beach now fully in view, below right. Where the track splits, keep right and then walk ahead with the wall boundary on your immediate left. A path through gorse leads out onto a tarmac lane that meanders ahead between detached housing.

Reach a large opening on the right, indicated with two public footpaths. Take the footpath on the right, passing through a wooden gate and descending towards the beach. Continue downhill before bearing left on a track just above the bottom cottage. Cross a small stream and follow the sandy coastpath. Continue adjacent to a wire fence, eventually retracing your earlier steps back to the car park.

WALK
1

DISTANCE
4
MILES

TIME
2
HOURS

MAP REF.
ORDNANCE
SURVEY
LANDRANGER
203
356
264

WALK
MODERATE
GRADE

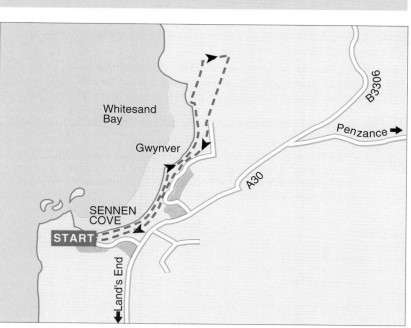

Whitesand Bay

Gwynver

SENNEN COVE

START

Land's End

B3306

Penzance ➡

A30

*Porth Chapel. MDN*

# PORTHCURNO AND PORTHGWARRA

*The landscape of the far south west around Porthcurno is some of the most stunning in Cornwall. Golden beaches, turquoise seas and granite cliffs make for an experience not easily forgotten. This walk heads west from Porthcurno, passing the world famous Minack Theatre before reaching the tiny fishing cove of Porthgwarra. From here, the coastal path passes around Gwennap Head before proceeding inland to follow field paths to the intriguing little church at St Levan.*

*Porthcurno was once the centre of world communications, following the laying of the first transatlantic phone cables to America in 1870. Guided tours around the museum here are available between April and October though it is advisable to ring first (01209 612142).*

**REFRESHMENTS & TOILETS**
Toilets at Porthcurno (start point) and Porthgwarra. Refreshments at Porthcurno.

**DIRECTIONS TO START**
From the A30 Penzance-Land's End road, turn onto the B3283 St Buryan road. Go through the villages of St Buryan and St Levan until you see the signs for Porthcurno. Continue down the hill to use the car park at the bottom.

## WALK DIRECTIONS

From the bottom of the car park, follow the track signed to Porthcurno Beach and coastpath. At a junction of paths, bear right (signed Porthgwarra) and follow the coastpath with Porthcurno Beach below to your left. After a short distance, ignoring the alternative route sign, follow the coastpath sign bearing right, climbing steps in the cliffside to pass just above the famous Minack Theatre, created by Rowena Cade in the 1920s. Proceed ahead to follow the coastal path through gorse and out towards the headland of Pedn-men-an-mere (take an optional detour here to enjoy the views, they are quite stunning).

Rejoin the coastal path to pass around the attractive and secluded beach at Porth Chapel. A small wooden footbridge is crossed before bearing right, initially inland and then to the left, uphill, at a signpost indicating the coastal path. The coastpath continues, with lovely sea views, before descending to the small fishing hamlet of Porthgwarra (toilets here).

Proceed on the coastpath away from Porthgwarra, keeping generally to the seaward side where there is the occasional path split. Walk past the coastal lookout station, ahead can be seen the granite cliffs of Land's End and the Longships Lighthouse.

Eventually descend to reach the granite bouldered cove of Porth Loe. From here, stay on the coastal path as it climbs away from the cove before reaching a stone wall and passing through it. Now bear to the right, following a path that leads towards a ruined cottage, a larger grey house further inland on the skyline. Leaving the coastal path behind, follow a faint path inland, the ruined cottage now ahead to the left. After a short while, a path through gorse reaches a track.

Bear right on this track and proceed through a metal gate, following the track between hedges to pass a large grey house. Walk on before turning left on to a concrete driveway. At the end of the driveway, turn right and walk past farm buildings, following the lane.

Where the word "SLOW" has been painted on the road surface, look for a public footpath signed on the left. Here, cross the stile and walk ahead keeping to the right hand side of the field. Cross a stile next to a metal gate and walk on through a further field to cross a further stile, St Levan Church tower now clearly visible ahead. Cross several further stiles and fields in the same direction before crossing a stile left, half way down a field, St Levan Church now very close. A small stile leads right just before a row of cottages before allowing access to the churchyard. This contains interesting old gravestones and the split stone of St Levan - local legend insists that the world will come to an end when the split in the stone is wide enough to ride a donkey between!

Leave the churchyard via the top left corner where there is a good example of a granite coffin stile (there is an ancient cross adjacent). Walk up the field, the field boundary to your immediate right, before passing over a stile at the top and crossing a larger field with an old cross next to the path. Go through a metal kissing gate and bear to the right between houses, following the lane back towards Porthcurno. At the Mariners Lodge Hotel, follow the road left back to the car park.

**WALK 2**

**DISTANCE**

**4**

**MILES**

**TIME**

**2.5**

**HOURS**

**MAP REF.**

ORDNANCE SURVEY LANDRANGER 203

**385 226**

WALK GRADE MODERATE

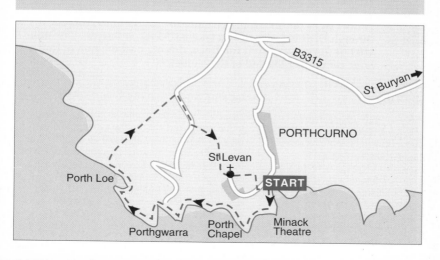

*Penberth Cove. MDN*

# TREEN, ST LOY'S AND PENBERTH COVE

*This area of West Cornwall provides classic coastal walking, facilitated by a myriad of inland paths which allow exciting circular routes to be constructed. Although St Ives, on the northern side of the peninsula, is famous for the quality of its light, this area offers a similar clarity of view, enhanced by pink and grey granite cliffs, turquoise seas and occasional sandy coves.*

**REFRESHMENTS & TOILETS**

Toilets, shop and pub at Treen (start point).

**DIRECTIONS TO START**

Follow signs on A30 from Penzance for Land's End. Proceed through Drift to Catchall and take B3283 for St Buryan. One mile after St Buryan, turn left for Treen, driving past the pub to find a large car park at the end of the hamlet.

## WALK DIRECTIONS

Walk out of the car park and down the road through the hamlet, passing the pub. At the road T-junction, turn right, walking downhill but ignoring the right turn signed to Penberth. Stay with the road, crossing the road bridge at the bottom before climbing steeply up the other side. Walk uphill to reach a sharp left bend and a farm entrance on the right (Boscean Farm). Do not bear right on the farm entrance, instead walk ahead, up steps, just to the left of the farm entrance (public footpath sign).

Pass over a stile and continue ahead, keeping to the right-hand side. In the top right corner pass up steps in the wall and then walk diagonally ahead towards farm buildings and trees. Pass through a gate in the far left corner and then turn immediate right through another gate. The public footpath leads diagonally across the field, in the direction of telegraph poles (if the field has just been ploughed and the path not reinstated, it may be easier to follow the field boundary left).

Cross the stile near to a telegraph pole and walk across the second field in the same manner. Pass up steps in the wall in the far right corner and cross right. Enter a field and walk along the bottom, the boundary on your immediate left. Pass over the boundary in the far left corner and down stone steps to reach a driveway. Turn left and proceed to reach a road.

Turn right and follow the road for a distance of just under three quarters of a mile. The road eventually descends, passing Lower Trevedran Farm and enters an area of trees. Just as the road starts to climb, turn right to take a public footpath signed near granite posts with an old metal gate. Follow the obvious woodland track, passing through a small gate. Cross a small stream via a large stone, keeping left at a path fork afterwards to recross the stream. An obvious path now leads down through the woods. In places, small diversions have been created around boggier areas and there are several fallen trees to be negotiated. The path eventually passes close to a stream before crossing via granite boulders and then bearing left down the opposite side.

Ignore a stile on the left (leading to St Loy's Cove) and walk out above a property to enjoy the coastal views. Follow the track ahead, bearing right to follow a broad grassy track between hedges (coastpath). This track climbs inland a little before bearing left on an obvious track near a

metal gate (coastpath waymark also). The coastpath is easily followed here and well waymarked - it is not long before the Logan Rock headland comes into view. Cross a stone stile and soon start to descend, using steps to pass near a boulder beach and over streams descending to the cove.

As indicated by the waymark, the coastpath climbs via steps away from the cove to provide level easy walking. It is now a case of staying on the coastpath to reach Penberth. En-route, cross a stile and keep left at two path forks reached shortly afterwards (coastpath waymarks). Descend to reach Penberth Cove.

Bear left across the granite bridge and walk in front of the restored capstan, used to pull boats up the slipway. Find a path leading uphill, adjacent to a small hut. The rocky path gradually climbs before levelling off to follow an obvious route through gorse and bracken. It is not long before you reach a T-junction in the path. Bear left if you wish to explore the Logan Rock headland, otherwise turn right and then take an immediate right (next to a small granite coin collection pyramid). An inland path leads up stone steps and crosses the field ahead on an obvious path. Cross two further stiles and fields in the same manner. Proceed through a third field and then bear left after a gate, following an unmade track. Where the track bears left, cross a stile ahead and bear right at the end to return to your car.

DISTANCE

4.5

MILES

TIME

2.5

HOURS

MAP REF.

ORDNANCE
SURVEY
LANDRANGER
203

395
228

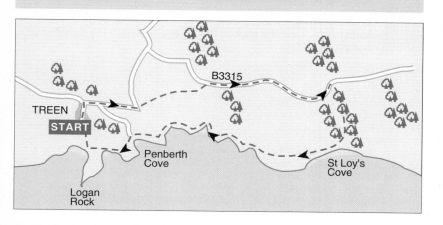

*Portheras Cove. MDN*

# PENDEEN WATCH, MORVAH AND PORTHERAS COVE

*Pendeen Watch Lighthouse, on the far north-western tip of Cornwall, provides the start point for a walk that combines inland field paths with an interesting ramble on the Cornish coastpath. The route also passes the attractive Portheras Cove, a secluded bathing spot of golden sand which unfortunately holds a deadly secret; the beach contains sharp metal fragments resulting from a dynamited shipwreck.*

*The lighthouse at Pendeen is no longer staffed full-time although thanks to the efforts of the Trevithick Trust, it is open to the public for tours (Apr-Oct, weekdays). The tours explore the engine room that provides power for the largest surviving fog signal in Britain.*

**REFRESHMENTS & TOILETS**

None encountered within the immediate course of the walk.

**DIRECTIONS TO START**

Pendeen village is located on the B3306, north of St Just, near Land's End. Take the road in the village signed to the lighthouse and park nearby.

## WALK DIRECTIONS

With your back to the lighthouse, walk back up the road on which you arrived. Pass a row of houses on the left and continue, gaining height and bearing right. Walk past a detached cottage on the left and stay on the road until reaching a road off to the right. Do not turn right here, instead turn left down a farm track. Just before a converted barn, follow a waymark indicating a right over a stile, the narrow path now leading up the side of the property. After a further stile, walk alongside the left of the field, crossing a stile and walking over the next field in the same direction.

At the next stile, follow the waymark indicating a left over a small field. Pass over a stile and now walk with the boundary on your right, crossing a stile to reach a tarmac lane. Bear left before crossing a stile on the right adjacent to a barn. At the end of the barn, cross the field half left, passing over a stile to the left of a gate. Walk down the field in the direction of the electricity pole, continuing on to find a gap in the scrub ahead. Pass down steps (slippery!) and cross a stream before climbing up the other side next to a small concrete building. Reach a broad track at the top. Turn right for approx. 10 yards and then bear left to climb up step stones in the wall. Walk ahead across the field towards farm buildings.

Cross a stile to the left of the farmhouse and walk straight ahead, through a metal gate and between barns. Immediately after the barns, bear right through a gate and then turn left, following the boundary on the left. Where the boundary bears right, cross a wall stile and follow the footpath across the field ahead (if just sown, follow the boundary left). Cross the wall stile ahead and then turn left to follow the field boundary. In the far left corner, cross a stile and walk ahead before bearing left to walk down the field with the boundary on the right. Pass over a stile in the bottom right corner and follow a marked path through a garden. A track passes adjacent to a house before turning right on a wide track in front of properties and out onto the road. Turn left here, taking care, as there is no path, and walk into the hamlet of Morvah.

Bear left on the first side road in the village (next to a converted Wesleyan Chapel) and proceed to find a small attractive church. Take the adjacent public footpath signed on the left, crossing a stile to follow a track. At the end of the church boundary wall, take a stile and walk between two hedges, crossing a stile and heading towards the sea. A granite stile is crossed before reaching a waymark with arrows and an acorn sign, an indication that you have reached the coastpath.

Turn left, crossing a stile and boggy area via step stones. A grassy path continues ahead, in part alongside a granite boundary wall. Cross a stile, the coastpath somewhat inland from its more usual cliffside position. The coastpath then crosses a boundary wall before continuing on, the top of Pendeen Light now coming into view. Descend over a boundary wall next to a waymark and bear right on a track that leads down towards Portheras Cove.

After crossing a stream, the coastpath climbs away from the cove using an obvious track that is easily followed. It is now just a case of continuing ahead before eventually reaching a large granite stile to the right of a gate. This leads to a rough track that returns to the lighthouse and start point.

WALK
4

DISTANCE
4
MILES

TIME
2
HOURS

MAP REF.
ORDNANCE SURVEY
LANDRANGER 203
380
357

WALK GRADE MODERATE

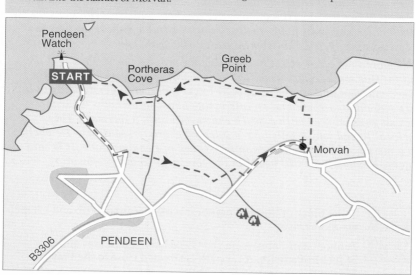

Pendeen Watch

START

Portheras Cove

Greeb Point

Morvah

PENDEEN

B3306

*Zennor. MDN*

# ZENNOR AND PENDOUR COVE

*Zennor is situated in the heart of the granite coastal plain that makes up the area of north Penwith, west of St Ives. This is a relatively isolated and at times, harsh landscape, with small hamlets nestling between the broken inland granite moors and dramatic sea cliffs. The area is well known to geographers and archaeologists for its Bronze Age field patterns; small fields enclosed with irregular granite borders that have changed little since their establishment over 2,000 years ago.*

*Although little more than a one street hamlet, Zennor provides more than just the starting point for this walk. Apart from the Wayside Museum, Cornwall's oldest privately owned museum and an essential visit to get a deeper understanding of this area, there is a pub and tea-room and an interesting house of worship. St Senara's Church houses an unusual seat with a bench end carved with a mermaid. This relates to the local legend which tells how a talented chorister, Matthew Trewhella, was lured by a mermaid to live with her on the seabed of Pendour Cove. It is said that their singing is sometimes still heard in the cove near to where you start this walk......*

**REFRESHMENTS & TOILETS**  Toilet block at the start point car park in Zennor. Pub and Chapel tea-rooms also.

**DIRECTIONS TO START**  Zennor (start point) is on the B3306 between St Ives and St Just-in-Penwith. A car park is situated close to the Wayside Museum.

## WALK DIRECTIONS

Walk towards the church, passing the pub on the left. Follow a sign indicating a path on the left to Zennor Head and the coastpath. A tarmac path runs to the left of farm buildings before heading towards the sea and passing a couple of detached properties. Cross a stone stile next to a National Trust sign for Zennor Head.

Turn left (signed Pendeen Watch), on the coastpath, descending steps with the aid of a handrail. A footbridge leads over a stream that runs to Pendour Cove (location for the mermaid legend). Keep to the main, boulder strewn coastpath, gradually climbing before levelling out to pass above Veor Cove, crossing a small stile.

The coastpath gradually descends as it leads away from Veor Cove. As you pass around the next headland, views open up towards Gurnard's Head, so named after its resemblance to the bulbous shaped head of the Gurnard fish. The coastpath climbs a little, adjacent to weathered stacks of granite, to reach a waymark post and path fork.

Now leave the coastpath, heading inland towards a granite house. Pass adjacent to the boundary wall and then follow the driveway track for just under half a mile. Pass through a gate and continue ahead at a track fork afterwards, climbing a little towards houses.

Pass a property on the left and then bear left to take a track that proceeds past attractive stone cottages on the left. After a short distance, leave the track to take a waymarked stile adjacent to a gate and telegraph pole (note the type of stile which is very common in this area). Walk adjacent to the left-hand side of the field, continuing in the same way in a second field. Walk past a metal gate, following the direction of the waymark arrow, to find a step stile further on in the boundary. Cross a third and fourth field, the tower Zennor Church now in sight. Cross two further fields and as indicated by a waymark next to a boundary wall, cross a stile, keeping to the left. A track leads between a wall and a hedge, crossing a stile next to a gate. Proceed ahead to reach the tarmac village road. Turn left and walk downhill back to the car.

WALK
**5**

DISTANCE

**2.5**

MILES

TIME

**1.5**

HOURS

MAP REF.

ORDNANCE
SURVEY
LANDRANGER
203

**455
384**

WALK
**MODERATE**
GRADE

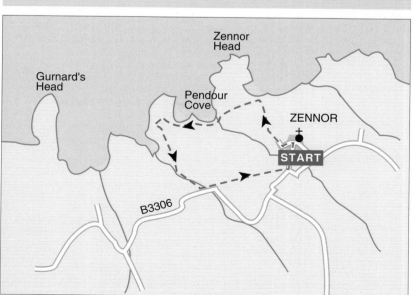

# TRENCROM HILL AND THE KNILL'S MONUMENT

*Lying to the south of St Ives, the 500ft. high heather covered summit of Trencrom Hill offers some of the best views in Cornwall. On clear days, both coasts can clearly be seen; Godrevy Lighthouse marking St Ives Bay to the north and east, the unmistakable St Michael's Mount and Mount's Bay, to the south.*

*From Trencrom, the walk strikes north to reach a further viewpoint at Knill's Monument, now well known for a obscure ceremony held in July every five years. The ritual involves a party of ten girls, each under ten years of age and daughters of tinners, seamen or fishermen, who must walk from central St Ives up to the fifty foot high triangular granite pyramid, accompanied by two elderly widows and a fiddler.*

**REFRESHMENTS & TOILETS**

None are encountered within the immediate course of the walk although the Tyringham Arms pub is near the start of the walk.

**DIRECTIONS TO START**

From the large roundabout on the western side of the Hayle by-pass, turn off for Lelant and bear first left (signed B3311 St Ives Day Visitors). After 1 mile, turn left (signed Cripplesease). For the start point, find a small N.T. parking area on the right (Trencrom Hill).

## WALK DIRECTIONS

Do not take the path leading from the back of the car park but instead walk back towards the road. Just before the car park entrance, turn left over a stile - an adjacent waymark post, marked with a stylised scallop shell, indicates it is part of St Michael's Way. This is a pilgrims' route between Carbis Bay, near St Ives, to St Michael's Mount, the waymarks will be seen on much of the first half of the walk. Follow the track - the top of Trencrom Hill, which will be encountered at the end of the walk, is above left. The track passes around the side of the hill, through a landscape of bracken and gorse, before eventually crossing a stile to reach a road opposite a farm gate.

Cross the road and go through the farm gate before bearing left and then immediate right, walking with the boundary on your right (there is an isolated stile here also). Walk down into the valley before bearing slightly left and passing over a stile next to a gate. Pass down steps and to the side of a converted property. Do not bear right on the driveway past the garage but instead proceed ahead, near a lamppost, to find a fairly well hidden track that leads down to the road. Cross the road to follow a St Michael's Way waymark, walking alongside a stream. Bear left at a wide track next to a cottage and proceed uphill. At the top of the track, bear right in front of a detached property and follow a narrow track, adjacent to the side of the house. Continue between high hedges to reach and

cross a stile. Follow the fenced edge of the field. Bear left over a stile and turn right, following the hedge boundary before crossing a stile right to reach a tarmac lane.

Cross the lane and take the first track on the left (St Michael's waymark). Bear right into a field next to a large granite rock just before farm buildings. Walk across the field and over a stile in the boundary ahead, following a short track before crossing a further stile to reach a caravan park. Walk ahead on a slightly left bearing to find a public footpath (a narrow track starting to the right of a shower block). Follow the track ahead over a stile to reach a lane.

Bear right for a few yards before taking the first track on the left, passing a large property situated on the right. Walk past Trewartha Farm before now following a narrower track, overgrown in parts, especially overhead. Walk out onto a driveway that serves cottages. After the first property on the left, turn left, following a track uphill. Bear right at the top, the track leading between cottages and on past other houses. Walk on to reach a T-junction at the end of the lane. Bear left and then almost immediately right, through a kissing gate signed as a public footpath (on the left is a stone house with outside staircase). Walk ahead, ignoring other paths, and continue in the same direction, eventually passing through a wooden kissing gate to reach a tarmac road.

Turn left, walking uphill and proceeding until

you find a tarmac path on the left, signed to Knill's Monument and adjacent to an information board. Turn left and walk up to enjoy the views from the monument. Standing with your back to the coat of arms on the monument, walk ahead towards a gate. Do not however pass through the gate, instead bear left on a narrow track (about 60 yards from the monument) and at a path fork, bear left as indicated by the St Michael's Way waymark. The track leads down to a tarmac road.

Turn left and walk along the road before taking the first road right (opposite a sign on the left for Vorvas Vean Farm). Follow the road between attractive cottages before turning left into Higher Vorvas Farm. Pass to the left of the main property and walk through a gate next to a stile. Cross the field ahead, bearing slightly right to use a stile near a small row of conifers. Bear right to walk ahead alongside the right-hand field boundary. Pass over the stile in the right-hand corner and cross the field ahead and over a stile. Descend down the next field, initially half right before then bearing left in front of a wooden fence to reach a stile with a public footpath sign (near a large granite boulder). The route leads over granite rocks and down steps to a driveway. Keep straight ahead, up steps on the opposite side to reach a waymark

next to a slate roofed building. Keep adjacent to this building and then bear left in front of the main house, following a driveway track downhill. Bear right away from stables to reach the road.

Turn left and cross to the other side (taking care as this road can be busy), now walking along the road. Pass a right turn signed to Trencrom and shortly afterwards find a footpath on the right (opposite a small road bridge). Take the footpath, climbing steps and over a stile. The public footpath leads directly uphill but if the field has just been sown, follow the field left and walk adjacent to the boundary. Pass through a gate gap in the top left corner, proceeding uphill on the left. Pass through a gate at the top and over granite rocks, keeping ahead on the left and through a muddy area at the top. Pass through a gate to reach a road.

Turn left and ignore a footpath on the right, walking past semi-detached houses on the left. Now note a stile on the right with a National Trust sign for Trencrom Hill. Take this stile and follow the obvious path uphill to the granite strewn summit. After enjoying the views, continue over the top and take a track that starts to descend with a view of St Michael's Mount directly ahead. The route passes around a huge boulder that seems to be balanced on a rock, before descending back to reach the car park.

WALK
6

DISTANCE
5
MILES

TIME
3
HOURS

MAP REF.
ORDNANCE SURVEY LANDRANGER 203
517
360

WALK
MODERATE
GRADE

*Warning: Parts of this route can be muddy.*

Knill's Monument

A3074

START

TRENCROM HILL

*The White Hart, Ludgvan. MDN*

# LUDGVAN AND THE ST MICHAEL'S WAY

*Ludgvan is a small village set in the farming country to the north of Penzance and Mount's Bay. It has a church and pub and employment is predominantly through agriculture, including flowers such as daffodils and carnations. There is a network of trails surrounding the village, some of which are used infrequently, leading to overgrown stiles and narrow pathways, best walked in long trousers! What the paths do have to offer however are stunning views across Mount's Bay to St Michael's Mount.*

*On parts of this walk you will see waymark posts signed with a stylised black scallop shell. This indicates St Michael's Way, a 12 mile route from Carbis Bay to St Michael's Mount. Like the Saints' Way between Padstow and Fowey, the way is part of a pilgrim route, used on the journey to St James' Cathedral in Santiago de Compostela, Spain.*

**REFRESHMENTS & TOILETS**

The White Hart Inn is at the start of the walk.

**DIRECTIONS TO START**

From the A30 at Crowlas near Penzance, take the B3309 signed to Ludgvan. Park in front of the church near the White Hart Inn.

## WALK DIRECTIONS

Walk up the steps and into the churchyard, bearing left around the church and out through the main gates. Turn right and at a telephone box, right again to follow a broad shady track marked as a public footpath. Ignore a public footpath on the left and walk ahead passing over a stone stile next to a gate. Descend through woodland and cross a small stream and adjacent stile.

Cross the field ahead on a half left bearing before passing over a stile. Walk up a shady lane, passing over a stile next to a gate to reach a tarmac lane. Turn left and after a short distance, turn right to pass over a stone stile near a metal gate. Walk adjacent to the left-hand field boundary, passing over a stile and following a well-defined path that proceeds diagonally down the field. Continue through an area of trees, crossing a stile and stream to reach an open field. Bear diagonally left to reach a stile at the top next to two gates - this is a tremendous viewpoint across Mount's Bay and St Michael's Mount. After the stile, walk up the field keeping to the left - a stile at its end leads you to a tarmac road.

Turn left and walk to find Boskennal Farm on the left-hand side. Turn left into the farmyard and walk straight ahead between two barns where there is a footpath sign. Go through a metal gate. The path bears left around the top of the barn before bearing right to reach a grassy open area. From here, take an overgrown path on the right and descend over a stile into woodland. In the right hand corner of the woodland, cross a stile and turn left to pass over a footbridge before emerging into an open field. Walk up the field, keeping to the right and pass over a stile next to a gate. Walk ahead, again on the right and at the top of the field, cross right over a stile, walking along the top of a field for just a few yards before crossing left over a stile to reach a wide track. Turn left and walk past two farmhouses to reach a tarmac road.

Cross the road and walk down the public footpath signed ahead. Pass a cottage on the left, over a stream and through a metal kissing gate. Walk on the slightly higher path that runs roughly parallel with the stream before gradually bearing to the right and passing through a large gap in the hedge boundary. Walk ahead and on reaching the open field, turn left

towards buildings (St Michael's Mount can be seen in the distance in line with the top of the roof). On reaching a garden fence, turn right and go over a wooden stile. Walk on the left before crossing a stile to reach a main road (B3309).

Turn left for ten yards before crossing the road and passing over a waymarked stile on the right. After a garden and a gate, go across a field and over a stile, walking on the right side of the field. As the field boundary starts to bear left, go past a gap in the hedge to reach an area of scrub on the right. Take a path across this area and follow the right edge of the field again. In the right hand corner, pass over an overgrown stile and through a small area of trees. After a further stile, take a half left path leading across the field to a stile and a tarmac lane.

Turn left and follow the lane, passing stone houses on the left. Immediately after passing a stone cottage on the right, turn right over a stone stile. Follow the right edge all the way around the field and up the other side to cross a stile on the right. Now proceed ahead, adjacent to the left-hand side. At the end of the field, bear left and after a stone stile, turn right to reach the B3309 again. Follow the road back to the church and your car.

DISTANCE
3.5
MILES

TIME
2.5
HOURS

MAP REF.
ORDNANCE SURVEY LANDRANGER 203
506
331

WALK GRADE MODERATE

Warning: Parts of this route can be muddy.

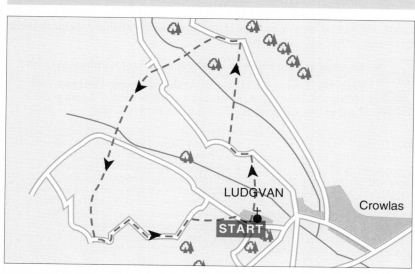
LUDGVAN

Crowlas

START

*Wheal Prosper engine house, Rinsey Head. MDN*

# RINSEY HEAD AND WHEAL PROSPER

*Rinsey Head is a small National Trust headland on the eastern side of Mount's Bay. It provides attractive coastal walking and on clear days panoramic views from St Michael's Mount around to Tater Du lighthouse near Mousehole can be enjoyed. Rinsey Head is principally known however for the mid nineteenth century engine house of Wheal Prosper tin and copper mine. The National Trust acquired the headland in 1969 and immediately set about restoring the unsafe chimney and capping the 600 foot deep shaft just in front of the engine house. A little further along the coast are the remains of engine houses belonging to the Wheal Trewavas copper mine dating from the 1830s and 1840s.*

*The route heads west initially from Rinsey to pass close to the popular bathing beach of Praa Sands. Waymarked paths across farmland and the occasional lane are then used to return to the coastpath east of Trewavas Head, facilitating an enjoyable coastpath walk back to the start point at Rinsey.*

**REFRESHMENTS & TOILETS**

En-route in Praa Sands in nearby Ashton (not within main walk).

**DIRECTIONS TO START**

From the A394 at the village of Ashton, between Penzance and Helston, follow signs for Rinsey (opposite Lion & Lamb pub). Park in the National Trust car park at Rinsey Cliffs.

## WALK DIRECTIONS

Return to the entrance of the car park, bearing left for five yards before heading right to follow the coastpath. Continue through the National Trust property of Lescleave Cliff, ahead can be seen the beach resort of Praa Sands. Stay on the coastpath, ignoring inland paths. The footpath descends, passing just above steps down to the beach, before reaching a parking area at the eastern end of Praa Sands.

Leave the parking area and turn left indicated by a coastpath sign onto a tarmac path that runs below houses. Walk ahead (ignore left turn indicating coastpath) until reaching a car park adjacent to a tennis court (Praa Sands Hotel). From here, follow the road as it bears right and walk uphill past the Post Office Stores. Pass Pengersick Castle on the left to reach a point where the road bears off to the left. Turn right (Pengersick Parc) and walk up a tarmac road to cross a stile at the top next to a metal gate. Follow a narrow path uphill and over a stile, eventually emerging to reach a tarmac road.

Turn left and walk through a small hamlet to reach a point where the road bears off to the left. Now cross a stone stile on the right and walk up the field keeping to the right hand side. Cross a stile in the top right corner and then walk ahead. After a further stile, follow a broad farm track before reaching a tarmac road. Turn right and after just a few yards, turn left in front of a stone cottage. Just before a metal gate, turn right across a stile and then walk staying adjacent to the left-hand field boundary. Views right are across Cudden Point towards Mounts Bay. Pass over a stile in the corner of the field and walk across a further field and stile. In the next field, keep to the right hand field boundary. Half way across the field, pass over a fairly overgrown stile and now walk with the hedge boundary on your left. Cross the stile ahead to reach a road and the hamlet of Rinsey.

Turn right and walk along the road before bearing left at a triangle of open land and proceed ahead towards a stone barn (on the right). Walk ahead over a stile and cross the field to a stepstile and then turn left, keeping the stone boundary wall to your left, walking in the same direction as before. Cross the next field diagonally to a gate and then walk straight across the next field to a stone stile in the hedge opposite. In the final field, keep the boundary wall to your left and cross another stone stile to reach a tarmac lane next to farm buildings.

Take the public footpath directly opposite, walking across a field with the farm buildings now on your right. Pass over a stile next to a wooden gate and cross the field diagonally to a stone stile half way along the opposite hedge (footpath sign). After this, walk on to pass over a stone wall via steps adjacent to a gate and proceed towards a farm. Pass to the left of the farm and then bear right following a broad track away from the farm. Pass through a gate and walk past an old barn to eventually reach a road.

Turn right and walk downhill to find the first tarmac lane on the right. Turn right and descend, bearing left away from a farmhouse, taking a track that leads under trees. Bear left in front of a metal field gate and follow a grassy path for a few yards before bearing right down to the coastpath. After reaching the coastpath, turn right. The coastpath zig zags uphill before eventually levelling out and passing above the remains of engine houses of Wheal Trewavas Mine. The coastpath finally meanders back into Rinsey Cliffs to the engine house of Wheal Prosper that can be seen ahead. From here, a broad track leads straight back to the car park.

WALK

8

DISTANCE

5.5

MILES

TIME

3

HOURS

MAP REF.

ORDNANCE
SURVEY
LANDRANGER
203

592
271

WALK GRADE MODERATE

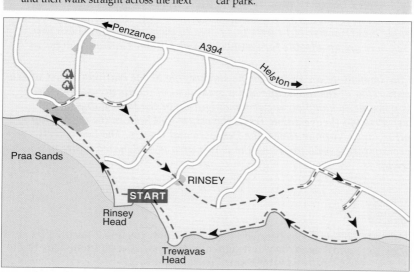

←Penzance

A394

Helston →

Praa Sands

RINSEY

START

Rinsey Head

Trewavas Head

*Porthleven Sands. MDN*

# LOE BAR AND THE LOE

*This route provides a short circular walk, ideal for families, using tarmac lanes and wide unmade tracks. It passes above Porthleven Sands and skirts the wide expanse of Loe Bar, a sand and shingle bank that has been formed by the sea. This has effectively dammed the small estuary of the River Cober to form Cornwall's largest natural lake, now known as The Loe (the Cornish 'logh' means pool). Whilst the sands provide an attractive but rarely busy area to picnic and relax, both the lake and the sea here are unsuitable for swimming and extreme caution is urged at all times.*

*The lake and the immediate area is under the safekeeping of the National Trust which has ensured protection of the landscape and a great deal of public access (for the energetic, it is possible to complete a circumnavigation of the lake, a distance of around 5 miles). Prior to the National Trust, the estate had been in the ownership of only two families since Norman times, the Penroses and Rogers. The Loe is well known for over-wintering wild fowl and the whole area is designated a Site of Special Scientific Interest.*

**REFRESHMENTS & TOILETS** — None.

**DIRECTIONS TO START** — Follow B3304 (signed Porthleven) from Helston. Shortly after an uphill bend, bear left signed to Loe Bar. Take an immediate left to use Penrose Hill National Trust car park.

## WALK DIRECTIONS

Walk out from the top of the car park and return to the road. Turn left and walk uphill before taking the first road left - signed to Loe Bar. Follow the road as it bears to the left, descending to reach the boundary wall of the Tye Rock Hotel. Here, bear left and walk down a lane (signed as dead end) to reach a small parking area. Now bear left to take a footpath to Loe Pool, signed through the National Trust property of Parc-an-als Cliff. Proceed along the coastline, the wide expanse of sand of Loe Bar becoming visible. The coastpath eventually reaches a large detached property. Here, do not descend right towards the beach, but continue directly ahead between granite posts. The broad track follows the edge of The Loe, passing through woodland and providing interesting lake views.

The route strikes inland to pass adjacent to the National Trust property of Penrose House. Follow the tarmac lane to the right, crossing between fertile meadows. At a T-junction, bear left (signed Porthleven) and walk uphill and over a large stone bridge. Follow the lane as it bears right. Where the lane bears sharply left, look for a waymarked path on the right, up steps, that leads through trees. Emerge to cross a tarmac road and pass through a gate to return to the car park from which you started.

DISTANCE
2.5
MILES

TIME
1.5
HOURS

MAP REF.
ORDNANCE
SURVEY
LANDRANGER
203
639
259

WALK
EASY
GRADE

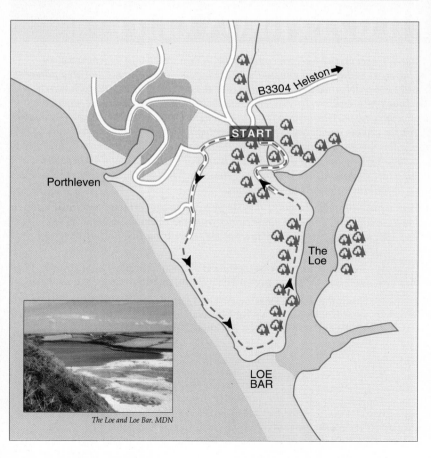

The Loe and Loe Bar. MDN

Gunwalloe Church Cove. MDN

# GUNWALLOE CHURCH COVE AND HALZEPHRON CLIFF

Gunwalloe Church Cove, on the western coast of the Lizard Peninsula, is renowned as having one of the most isolated and unusually sited churches in Cornwall. Located adjacent to the beach and with a detached bell tower dug into the cliff side, St Winwaloe Church dates from the fourteenth century. Its existence results from the once large and prosperous settlement that was here, particularly in the tenth and eleventh centuries - the Domesday entry of 1086 for the area is one of the largest in Cornwall. More recent historical events however provide the reason behind the area's alternative name of Dollar Cove. In 1527 the St Anthony, a Portuguese treasure ship was wrecked here and in the late eighteenth century a Spanish ship also met its fate just to the north of the cove. The lure of riches has resulted in many attempts to find the treasure but to no avail.

The walk follows a path through the golf course before continuing on road and field paths to reach the Halzephron Inn. This unusual name comes from the Cornish 'als' and 'yfarn' meaning 'Hell's Cliff', a reference to the centuries of shipwrecks on this part of the coast.

**REFRESHMENTS & TOILETS**  Both at start point (refreshments seasonal, toilets year round). Pub and teas (at Halzephron Herb Farm) available near end of walk.

**DIRECTIONS TO START**  From the A3083 Helston to The Lizard road, follow signs from near RNAS Culdrose for Gunwalloe. Follow road for approx. three miles and use the large National Trust car park near the beach.

### WALK DIRECTIONS

Leave the car park via the far right corner and turn left on a tarmac lane. Pass the toilet block and shop, keeping left on a wider tarmac road that heads towards the beach. Shortly before the end of the road, turn left on a sandy path that leads across a stone bridge and proceeds ahead, uphill, across a golf course. At the end of the track, pass to the left of the clubhouse to reach a road.

Turn left and cross to walk up the side of the road, taking care as this road is busy and there is no path. Walk for a little under three quarters of a mile to reach the hamlet of Cury. Take the first road left (signed Milliwarne). Walk past a graveyard and on to find a stone stile on the left, adjacent to a large gate and telegraph pole. Cross the stile and field ahead in the direction of farm buildings. Walk through a gate and follow the driveway towards Sowanna Farm. Bear left in front of the farmhouse.

After a short distance, bear right off the main track (public footpath sign) to reach a step stile with a waymark post. Head downhill, keeping to the right. When the boundary bears off to the right, continue in the same direction and follow the boardwalk over a marshy area. Cross three stiles close to each other, after the last one, proceed ahead uphill following the obvious path. Pass over a stone stile in the boundary ahead. A fairly overgrown path leads to a further marshy area, crossed by boardwalks and stiles. Emerge to follow the path across the bottom of a meadow and take a stone and wooden stile. Now walk uphill before taking a track

indicated by a waymark post that runs alongside a hedge on the left. This leads to a shady track before crossing a stile next to a farm gate. Follow the track as it bears right, downhill, and cross a stile left at the bottom (quite muddy at times). Cross the open field ahead, heading for the right hand corner. Traverse a stile adjacent to a gate and follow a fairly overgrown lane, gradually uphill to reach a road.

Turn right and walk past the Halzephron Inn before taking the first road left. Descend on a slightly left bearing to follow a wide track, the beach below right. Pass a detached house and past a sign indicating the National Trust property of Baulk Head. Follow the now obvious coastpath, passing Halzephron Herb Farm (refreshments in season). Pass close to the road before following a broad tarmac track, bearing right at a small parking area to follow the coastpath along Halzephron Cliff. The coastpath eventually returns to the road at Gunwalloe, bear left to return to your car.

DISTANCE

**4.5**

MILES

TIME

**2.5**

HOURS

MAP REF.

ORDNANCE SURVEY LANDRANGER 203

**658**
**228**

WALK MODERATE GRADE

Warning: Parts of this route can be muddy.

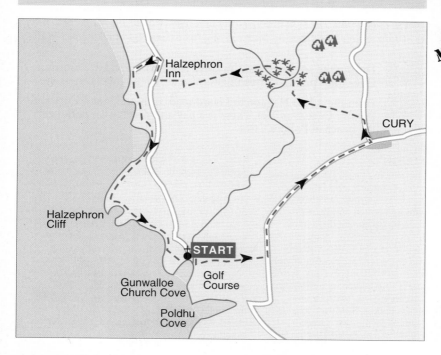

Halzephron Inn

CURY

Halzephron Cliff

START

Golf Course

Gunwalloe Church Cove

Poldhu Cove

*Polurrian Cove. MDN*

# POLDHU COVE AND MULLION

*The family bathing cove of Poldhu, on the western side of the Lizard Peninsula, is an attractive place to relax and picnic. The cove is now in the ownership of the National Trust which has carried out extensive improvement works, including sand-dune restoration and marram grass planting, to make it the enjoyable area it is today. Land to the south of the cove is also owned by the Trust since it was given by the Marconi Company in 1937. Poldhu Wireless Station was in operation here between 1900 and 1933 and a monument commemorates that it was from here that the first ever signal was conveyed across the Atlantic by wireless telegraphy. The signal, consisting of a repetition of the Morse letter 'S', was received at St Johns, Newfoundland by Marconi and his associates in December 1901.*

**REFRESHMENTS & TOILETS**

During the season at Poldhu Cove (start point) and at Polurrian Cove (mid point). Refreshments also at several hotels en-route.

**DIRECTIONS TO START**

From the A3083 Helston to Lizard road, turn off signed Cury and Poldhu Cove (3 miles). There is a pay and display car park near the beach at Poldhu Cove.

### WALK DIRECTIONS

Walk out of the car park back to the main road and bear left before turning right between stone posts to follow a tarmac drive marked with a footpath sign (toilets are situated below right on the beach). Follow the drive uphill with Poldhu Cove below right. Ignore the right turn signed for the coastpath (this will form part of the end of the walk) and continue uphill to approach the old Poldhu Hotel. Just as you reach the parking area in front of the building, follow the direction of a footpath sign for Mullion and bear to the left between granite posts. This leads to a wide gravel track between fields. After a stone stile, the track

bears both to the right and then left, passing Seven Pines on the left and then following the lane past bungalows.

After passing a large barn and an attractive thatched cottage, pass through a gate on the right hand side (just as the lane starts to bear away to the left), noting an adjacent stone commemorating the presence here of John Wesley in 1762. Walk directly across the field before crossing a stile and using a fairly overgrown path. After a further stile, follow a waymarked path across a meadow. Do not take the public footpath marked adjacent to the electricity pole but instead bear left to pass to the side of a large wooden gate and walk up a short lane between houses to reach a tarmac road. Cross the road, through a gate and walk ahead up a track between gardens to reach the main road.

Turn right and walk on to take the first road on the right (Laflouder Lane). Ignore the first turn right (Meres Valley). Just before a low thatched cottage (Laflouder Thatch), bear left with a long stone barn on the left. Pass below houses before continuing on a track between hedges and emerging on to a road. Now turn right and follow the road through a housing estate to reach a T-junction. Turn left and walk back to reach the main road (B3296).

Turn right and cross the road to walk on the pavement on the other side. Passing Trenance Farm and keeping to the main road, look out for concrete steps with a metal handrail on the right-hand bend. Climb the steps and pass over the stile at the top. Walk around the field staying close to the right-hand hedge boundary. Cross the stile in the top right corner of the field and walk ahead, now keeping the fence boundary on the left. Cross the stile ahead and follow a rough track to the rear of a large property. Cross a further stile and walk between a hedge and a fence, crossing a stile to reach a tarmac road near the Mullion Cove Hotel.

If you wish to visit the attractive National Trust maintained harbour of Mullion Cove, bear left here and follow coastpath signs to the cove before retracing your route back to this point. To continue the walk, bear right to take the coastpath (acorn sign) adjacent to a National Trust sign for Polurrian Cliff. Pass the old coastguard lookout and follow the coastpath above cliffs. The coastpath then makes use of a wide unmade track, passing a detached double garage and houses before reaching a tarmac road. Bear left and follow a track (marked as coastpath) that gradually descends, passing underneath a footbridge. Shortly afterwards, where there is a fork in the track, keep left and pass down steps to reach Polurrian beach.

Cross the wooden footbridge and climb away to the left, following the coastpath, which is soon once again above cliffs. A National Trust sign indicates the path passes through Meres Cliff. The coastpath eventually reaches the Marconi Monument.

The coastpath now passes alongside the old Poldhu Hotel encountered earlier and uses steps to reach the driveway used at the start of the walk. Turn left and follow the lane downhill and back to your car.

## WALK 11

**DISTANCE**

4

**MILES**

**TIME**

2

**HOURS**

**MAP REF.**

ORDNANCE SURVEY LANDRANGER 203

666
200

WALK EASY GRADE

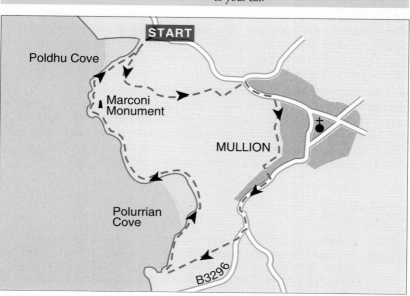

START

Poldhu Cove

Marconi Monument

MULLION

Polurrian Cove

B3296

*Gew-graze. MDN*

# PREDANNACK AND KYNANCE FARM NATURE RESERVE

*This walk explores the south western coastline of the Lizard Peninsula, an area regarded as of national and international importance. The landscape supports a variety of flora and fauna including the Cornish Heather, not found anywhere else. This as a result of the underlying geology of schists; hard, ancient rock formations created deep in the earth's crust before earth movements brought it closer to the surface.*

*The walk heads south from the National Trust car park at Predannack, passing through a heatherclad landscape and conservation area. Just to the east is Predannack Airfield, now used for training and glider flights but previously a World War Two fighter base for Spitfires and Hurricanes. The route reaches the coastpath at Gew-graze, just to the north of where the Spanish Armada galleons were first spotted in Britain back in July 1588. The coastpath then heads north over high cliffs to return to Predannack.*

**REFRESHMENTS & TOILETS**  None.

**DIRECTIONS TO START**  From the A3083 Helston to Lizard road, take the B3296 through Mullion following signs for Mullion Cove. Just before the road descends to Mullion Cove, take a left turn signed for Predannack. Continue for some distance before crossing a cattle grid to reach a National Trust car park.

## WALK DIRECTIONS

Leave the car park via a track at the bottom, walking between buildings (sign indicates cars prohibited). Pass over a stile next to a large farm gate and walk ahead on a grassy path to proceed over a second, smaller stile. Now follow the broad stony track ahead (ignoring footpath to cliff on right and footpath on left indicated with a blue waymark). Pass through a farm gate and after a few yards, go over a stile on the right hand field boundary before turning immediately left, walking between a hedge and a fence. Carry on over a stile at the end of the path and walk on to find a junction of paths. Do not continue ahead but instead turn right and cross a stile next to a large farm gate.

From here, a path leads ahead on a half right bearing through brambles and scrub. After a gate, an English Nature sign indicates you have reached the National Nature Reserve of Kynance Farm. Continue walking straight ahead; in the far distance can be seen farm buildings. At the end of the heathland area, walk on keeping to the left-hand boundary. Half way up the field and as indicated by a waymark, pass left through a gap in the hedge and then turn immediate right to walk with the field boundary now on your right.

The path leads across a gravel driveway before continuing towards the farm building top right. Pass through a large gate and follow the track which bears right, the farmhouse now above right. When the farmhouse is clearly in view, leave the wider track which starts to gain height towards telegraph poles and follow a grassy path to the right of the track that heads down the valley. This follows a small stream down to the sea.

At the coastpath just before a cove, turn right and follow the path steeply uphill before crossing over a stile next to a gate. Now follow the coastpath above towering cliffs for some distance. Cross two stiles en-route, before following the coastpath through a gate gap to walk alongside a hedge boundary on the right hand side. Soon after this look for a plaque in the hedge on the right concerning the Collins family. Approx. 25 yards further on, take a path bearing right, away from the coastpath (a National Trust sign for Predannack is on the left). Follow this path inland, passing over a stile before reaching the track used earlier. Turn left and take the little path accessed by stiles next to the main track before walking ahead back up to the car park.

DISTANCE
**3.5**
MILES

TIME
**1.5**
HOURS

MAP REF.
ORDNANCE SURVEY LANDRANGER 203
**669**
**161**

WALK EASY GRADE

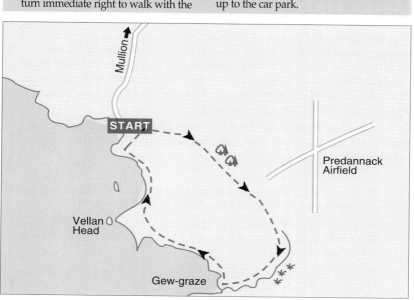

Mullion

START

Predannack Airfield

Vellan Head

Gew-graze

*Looking towards Kynance Cove from Predannack. MDN*

# KYNANCE COVE AND THE LIZARD

*Kynance Cove is rightly known as one of the most beautiful parts of Cornwall and has been a popular destination for visitors since Victorian times. Multicoloured serpentine rocks, turquoise seas and golden sands at low tides make the cove popular with bathers and families; the rich flora and fauna of the surrounding landscape a favourite with naturalists and walkers. This walk starts from Kynance Cove car park allowing an exploration of the cove after the walk.*

*The route follows inland paths to reach Lizard village, England's most southerly. From here a track joins the coastpath which provides stunning sea views all the way back to your start point.*

**REFRESHMENTS & TOILETS**
Seasonal refreshments and toilets at Kynance car park (start point). Year round facilities in Lizard village (mid point).

**DIRECTIONS TO START**
From the A3083 Helston to Lizard road, turn off following brown National Trust signs to Kynance Cove half a mile north of Lizard village.

## WALK DIRECTIONS

Leave the car park by the road on which you arrived. Continue along the road to pass a house (Carn Goon) on your right. Where the road bears left shortly after the house, leave the road and walk ahead to cross a stile (public footpath sign). Cross the field ahead and over two further stiles, following a path between bushes and scrub. A short avenue of trees leads to a further stile, the path now running along the top of a raised Cornish hedge. At the end of this, follow a wide track ahead before continuing on a tarmac road, with houses on either side, to reach the main Lizard village parking area.

Pass the toilet block on the right and walk ahead near hotels and a chip shop. Turn right immediately after the Top House pub, following the road as it proceeds past a post office. Continue along Penmenner Road. At the end of the road, adjacent to Penmenner House Hotel, continue down a stony track marked as a public footpath. This track leads to a public bridleway (marked for Pistol Meadow) which gradually descends to reach the coastpath next to a small wooden footbridge.

Turn right and follow the coastpath that leads back to Kynance Cove, crossing occasional stiles and gates. In places there are several paths but they all join up and reach a National Trust post. Ignoring the beach directions and following the acorn will return you to the Kynance Cove start point car park.

WALK
**13**

DISTANCE
**3.5**
MILES

TIME
**1.5**
HOURS

MAP REF.
ORDNANCE
SURVEY
LANDRANGER
203
**688**
**133**

WALK EASY GRADE

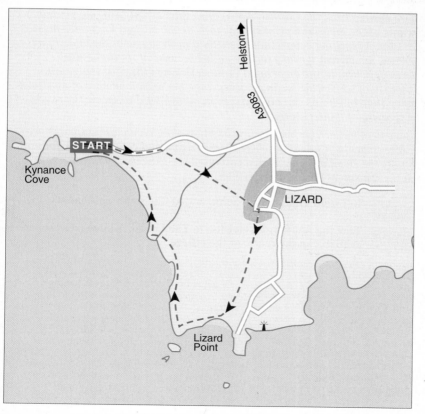

*Cadgwith. MDN*

# THE LIZARD, CHURCH COVE AND CADGWITH

*The name Lizard derives from the Cornish words "lis" (place) and "ard" (high) and refers to the whole of the moorland peninsula as well as the village, England's most southerly, at its tip. A reptilian connection exists only in the name of the underlying geology, serpentine, an ancient igneous rock so called because of its snakeskin appearance when polished. In the archetypal Cornish fishing village of Cadgwith, cottages built partly of serpentine are in evidence, together with a number of dwellings constructed using thatch. Chains can also be seen in places, used to secure the eaves, indicating the severity of winter storms.*

*The route follows field paths from the gloriously situated St Wynwallow Church near Church Cove. After reaching Cadgwith where there is a pub and café, the walk follows the coastpath past the Devil's Frying Pan, a collapsed sea cave with a narrow arch through which the sea surges when tides are high.*

**REFRESHMENTS & TOILETS**

In Lizard village (start point) and at Cadgwith (mid point).

**DIRECTIONS TO START**

Take the A3083 from Helston to The Lizard. A large free car park is available in the centre of the village.

## WALK DIRECTIONS

Stand in the centre of Lizard village (with your back to the Top House pub) and head along Beacon Terrace (i.e. opposite). As you walk along the road, the Lizard Lighthouse can be seen over the hedge to your right. Continue until reaching a right-hand road junction signed for Church Cove and the Lifeboat Station (next to an old stone cross). Take this road and walk for about half a mile to reach St Wynwallow Church.

Pass through the churchyard gate and walk to the left of the main tower, the path leading down a couple of steps to a wider track. Turn left along the track, walking between high hedges. Cross the stile at the end and walk ahead enjoying sea views on the right. Follow the path as it bears to the left, walking with a small valley below right. Look for a gap in the bracken near the head of the valley (this is quite overgrown and may take a while to find but is located by bearing right after a large area of bracken and is about half way down the field).

Pass down steep stone steps (slippery - take care!) and bear left after crossing the stream and a further left when the route meets a wider path. Reach a stone stile in the top corner of the field.

Turn right walking up the right hand side of the field. Cross a further stile and walk on to cross a third stile before bearing left along a broad track towards Trethvas Farm. Continue on the concrete track and then bear right in front of the farmhouse (public footpath sign to Cadgwith and Ruan Minor). Walk up a stile next to a gate and then follow the path along the top of a raised stone hedge, the radar dishes of Goonhilly Earth Satellite Station can now be seen to the left of Grade Church ahead. After passing down stone steps, follow the path ahead to cross a stile next to a gate.

Turn left on a tarmac road and walk until you reach a public footpath sign on the right indicated for St Grada Church. Pass through the large gate and use a wide grassy path to reach the church. Enter the churchyard via a stile and follow the path past the church door to reach a stile in the corner that provides access to a path down the side of the field. Proceed ahead, keeping the field boundary on the left and ignoring a stile in the left corner of the field. Instead, continue to the next field corner and take a stile that leads to a stone path between hedges. Pass

through a kissing gate and across a field ahead to reach a gate and a road.

Cross the road to reach Methuven Farm. Keep left, following a tarmac lane (signed for Cadgwith) that proceeds past houses. This lane gradually descends to reach Cadgwith. When you are ready to leave the village, follow a path that leads to steps uphill next to a thatched cottage on the road bend (on the southern side of the village - the direction in which you first arrived). Emerge on a road and take a stile that indicates a public footpath leading up through the attractive gardens at Hillside. After the gardens, walk straight ahead before bearing left at a sign for Inglewidden and the Devil's Frying Pan.

You are now on the coastpath that leads around the spectacular collapsed sea cave. Few directions are now needed as it is simply a case of following the coastpath, crossing occasional stiles, before descending to reach Church Cove.

At Church Cove, bear right and walk uphill past attractive thatched properties (a gate on the left provides access to a road leading to the Lifeboat Station which is sometimes open to the public - note access to the station is via a long steep staircase). Continue on the lane past St Wynwallow Church and retrace your earlier route back along Beacon Terrace to the car park.

DISTANCE
4.5
MILES

TIME
2.5
HOURS

MAP REF.
ORDNANCE
SURVEY
LANDRANGER
203
704
126

WALK
EASY
GRADE

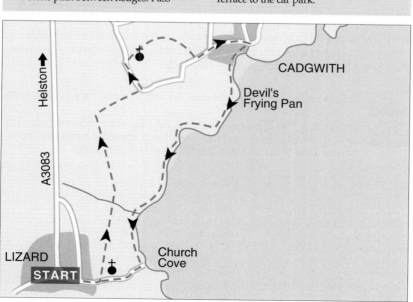

Helston

A3083

LIZARD

START

CADGWITH

Devil's
Frying Pan

Church
Cove

*Carleon Cove, Poltesco. MDN*

# POLTESCO, RUAN MINOR AND CADGWITH

*The Lizard Peninsula is unlike anywhere in Cornwall, with its broad heather covered plateau, home to a rich variety of flora and fauna. Also found here are large deposits of serpentine, a hard rock, usually red or green in colour, that responds to polishing, particularly fashionable in Victorian times for use in shop fronts and fireplaces. A flourishing industry grew up in the late nineteenth century, surviving today on a much smaller scale, although traces of a much larger and prosperous industry can still be found. One such place is at Poltesco, north of Cadgwith where this walk commences. The National Trust now largely owns the area which includes a three-storey warehouse, dating from 1866, providing an interesting end to this walk.*

**REFRESHMENTS & TOILETS**
Toilets and shop at Ruan Minor. Toilets, pub and café at Cadgwith.

**DIRECTIONS TO START**
From the A3083 Helston -Lizard rd, take the Ruan Minor/Cadgwith turn. In Ruan Minor, next to a school and opposite a bus shelter, a narrow lane leads down to the Poltesco N.T. car park.

## WALK DIRECTIONS

Proceed out of the car park the way you drove in, walking up the tarmac lane before bearing left and passing over a bridge. Continue up a steep hill to Ruan Minor. At the T-junction in the village, walk ahead to take a tarmac path located to the right of a bus shelter/phone box, passing a toilet block. At the road, turn right.

Where the road bears left to Cadgwith, continue straight on, passing a Methodist church and walk downhill. Take the stone steps and follow a gravel path past large detached houses. Cross a stile and walk around a field edge and over a further stile before bearing left down a wider track to reach a tarmac road.

Turn right and after only a short distance, look for a public footpath sign on the left, shortly after B&B accommodation. Follow the path, crossing a bridge and stile and then walk straight ahead, up the field. Head for the left-hand side of the farm buildings and in the corner pass through a metal gate, walking on a shady path before bearing right along a driveway. Turn left down a tarmac lane and immediately after passing a property named 'The Orchard', proceed through a gate on the left and across a field to reach the tiny holy well of St Ruan.

Bear left in front of the well, following a very short and fairly overgrown path that leads over an adjacent stile to a road. Turn left and stay on the road, ignoring public footpath signs and two roads on the right, one of which is signed to Cadgwith. The road descends to reach a public footpath on the right, with a serpentine stile, just before a bridge. Turn right across the stile and follow a wide shady path, straight ahead, down the valley into Cadgwith, passing the main Cadgwith car park on the way.

At the village, turn left and walk down to explore the cove. When you are ready to leave, follow the road past the pub on the left and start to walk away from the cove. Look for a coastpath sign sited on the left (just after the thatched Veneth Cottage), this leads to the coastpath heading away from Cadgwith. Pass the small black building that was formerly a coastguard lookout and now follow the coastpath, enjoying the far-reaching sea views.

Continue walking until reaching a wooden kissing gate. Immediately after, turn right over a stone step stile and then turn left with the field hedge on your left. The occasional stile will be encountered. After a kissing gate adjacent to a wooden gate with a path junction immediately after, keep right and descend towards Poltesco. This path proceeds between hedges before passing through a gate and descending to reach a path junction and the National Trust sign for Poltesco. Here, turn right and proceed down steps to take an opportunity to visit Carleon Cove where there was once a flourishing pilchard fishery and serpentine works. To return to your car, retrace your steps and bear right after crossing back over the footbridge, following the path past a house and up a driveway. Pass over a large wooden footbridge and turn right through the gate into the car park.

WALK
**15**

DISTANCE
**3**
MILES

TIME
**1.5**
HOURS

MAP REF.
ORDNANCE SURVEY LANDRANGER 204
**728 157**

WALK EASY GRADE

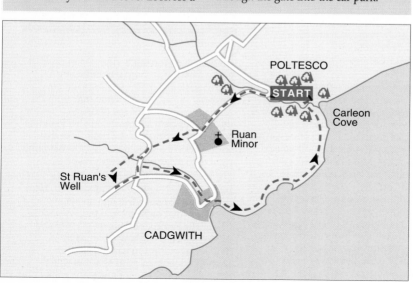

POLTESCO

START

Carleon Cove

Ruan Minor

St Ruan's Well

CADGWITH

# COVERACK, CHYNHALLS POINT AND BLACK HEAD

*This is a long and at times strenuous walk that explores the impressive coastal landscape on the eastern side of the Lizard Peninsula. It is an area of high granite cliffs, of gorse and heather and of stunning sea views.*

*The walk allows the exploration of the promontory of Chynhalls Point, just to the south of the attractive coastal fishing village of Coverack, a favourite with visitors. The coastpath is then used to pass around Black Head before field paths and country lanes complete the circular route.*

**REFRESHMENTS & TOILETS**

Both at Coverack (start point).

**DIRECTIONS TO START**

From the A3083 near RNAS Culdrose, south of Helston, follow signs for St Keverne (B3293). After a few miles, bear right and proceed on the B3294 into the village of Coverack. The main car park is found on the right near the entrance to the village.

## WALK DIRECTIONS

Turn right out of the car park and head downhill towards the sea. Follow the road right towards Coverack harbour. Enter the small parking area just past the Paris Hotel. Follow signs for the coastpath on the right, walking up beside the hotel. Immediately alongside a slate hung building, turn right and walk up steps (the path ahead leads to the sea only). At the top of the steps bear left and walk along a road to take the coastpath signed just to the left of a Wesleyan Chapel. Walk between cottages and attractive gardens before bearing left in front of a three-storey house (coastpath sign).

Continue ahead, keeping left at a path fork shortly after a concrete bench, heading towards Chynhalls Point. A meeting of paths next to a waymark post provides the opportunity to divert left and explore/picnic etc on the headland. After this or if you do not wish to make the diversion, take the coastpath route that leads uphill. Walk past a gate marked "private", gradually climbing to pass up wooden steps near a large hotel. As indicated by the waymark, follow a grassy path in front of buildings (there is also a row of granite blocks). This leads on to a tarmac driveway before turning left, signed as a public footpath to Black Head.

Pass to the left of a large bungalow and

*Coverack. MDN*

continue between tall hedges. At an open grassy area, keep sharp left, following a shady track and over a small stream via stepping stones. After a stone stile, with the sea now visible on the left once again, follow the obvious path to emerge on a wide farm track next to a gate on the right. Take this wide track for a short distance before bearing right onto a narrow path once again.

The obvious path leads ahead to pass a National Trust sign for Chynhalls Cliff. Here the coastpath passes through an open landscape that provides good views back to Chynhalls Point. Continue over a stile and footbridge before following an, at times, rocky course. Prior to passing an old coastguard lookout post, a further stile is encountered before continuing the walk around Black Head. The coastpath now follows a route closer to the cliff before eventually crossing a stile and entering the National Trust property of Beagles Point. A small wooden cross, found on the left, is a memorial to a crew member killed in a helicopter crash.

Cross a wooden footbridge, the coastpath now climbing before levelling out and heading towards Downas Cove. Go over a stile and descend into a wide valley behind the cove, crossing a stile and footbridge at the bottom. Ascend away from the cove, crossing two stiles, and walking next to a boundary fence. After a further stile, note the headland of Carrick Luz, below left. Continue on, crossing a further stile to reach a clearing near the neck of the headland.

Here, leave the coastpath by turning right through a gate and keeping to the left, walk uphill. Follow the unmade track as it bears right and then left, between hedges. Pass through a large metal gate and continue on the driveway ahead. Bear left to follow a tarmac road, continuing until reaching a T-junction. Turn right, walking over a bridge and through a small hamlet, eventually

passing a large granite farmhouse on the left. After this, walk past two gates on the right and stay on the road to find and take a public footpath on the right (adjacent to where the road is wider).

The shady path proceeds ahead to reach a tarmac road. Turn right following a no through road signed to Trewillis and Treleaver. Follow this quiet country road, ignoring the right turn and walking on to reach Trewillis Farm on the left. Just before the farm, take an overgrown path on the left and over a stile. Bear right along the field boundary before bearing to the left of farm buildings. Immediately after the buildings, bear right through a gate and then turn right on a wide cow track for a few yards to find a stile on the left. Cross the stile and field ahead on a half-left bearing. Cross a second stile and field and pass over a stile to the left of a telegraph pole. Bear half right across the next field to a further stile. Now take a right bearing, passing through a gap in the hedge and continuing across the field towards a gate.

Turn right on the road and walk back down into Coverack. Proceed back around the harbour and beach to return to the start point car park.

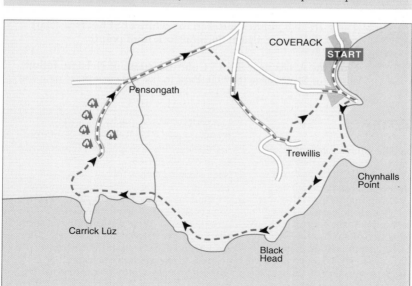

37

*Cottage, Porthoustock. MDN*

# ST KEVERNE AND PORTHOUSTOCK

*This route provides for an attractive walk through lush countryside, starting at St Keverne Church, site of many graves relating to shipwrecks caused by the treacherous Manacles Rocks. From here, the route proceeds to Porthoustock; the pebble beach at this coastal village is used as a starting point for offshore divers and makes for the midpoint of this walk for those looking for a relaxing spot from which to gaze at the sea.*

**REFRESHMENTS & TOILETS**

There are two public houses in the centre of St Keverne (start point). Toilets are also at Porthoustock (mid point).

**DIRECTIONS TO START**

From the A3083 near RNAS Culdrose, south of Helston, follow signs for St Keverne (B3293). Park in the village square near the church.

## WALK DIRECTIONS:

Head through the church gate (notice memorial stone on the wall to the right) and bear left in front of the church. Follow a tarmac path straight ahead through the graveyard, passing alongside a wall before going through metal and wooden kissing gates. Walk ahead with the hedge to your left (the sea can be seen on the horizon) before continuing over a stone stile and now walking with the hedge on the right. At the end of the field, cross a concrete driveway via two stiles and walk ahead between two hedges. Continue to follow the hedge boundary on the left. Where it ends, proceed in the same direction, gradually descending to cross a stile ahead.

After stepping stones, follow the obvious path between hedges. The route passes over a footbridge before continuing just to the left of a stream through an attractive wooded area (the path is presently blocked by a fallen tree but can be negotiated by the able!). After a cattle grid like stile, bear right along a shady track signed to Porthoustock. Eventually reach a tarmac lane. Turn left and just after an attractive cottage on the left, find a public footpath sign on the right.

Cross a small stream and adjacent stile before walking ahead to follow an obvious path that proceeds just to the right of trees. Pass up steps and on through a metal kissing gate. Continue to a stile and walk in front of attractive thatched cottages to reach the road that leads down to Porthoustock (a nice place to picnic although the beach is made up of stone, shale and shingle).

From the beach at Porthoustock, retrace your route back up the road. Do not walk back alongside the cottages but instead stay with the road and walk uphill. Pass Chyreen Farm on the right and stay with the road to pass through the small hamlet of Trenance. Ignore the left turn signed to Trenoweth Mill and walk uphill to a junction. As indicated by a coastpath waymark, cross the junction to take a stile leading to a route between hedges. Pass over a stile (a vineyard is on the left) and after steps, follow a concrete driveway to the right of a farm. Pass through two gates to reach a tarmac road.

Turn right and descend to the point where the road bears right, next to the Porthallow village sign. Bear left (unless you have plenty of time and wish to visit the village and pub) and follow the public footpath through an area of woodland. Cross a stile next to a gate and continue on before emerging into an open field. Bear left

and cross a stile, following a track between two hedges. After a small stream, bear uphill, passing to the left of Tregaminion Farm.

Turn left in front of the farmhouse before leaving the driveway to take a public footpath signed to St Keverne on the right. A gate leads to an open field. Bear left after the barn to cross a stile next to a gate. Walk ahead on a half right bearing to cross a stone stile in the right-hand field boundary. The height gained provides views behind you across Falmouth Bay. Walk with the field boundary on your right and after a stone stile in the right hand corner, cross the field ahead, St Keverne Church spire acting as your guide. Cross a further stile and small field before passing over another stile to reach a road.

Turn right and after only 25 yards, turn left over a waymarked stile. Walk beside the hedge on the right and after a stile, continue in the same direction to reach a fork in the path in the bottom right corner. Keep left and pass down steps before crossing two stiles. A partly made lane now proceeds away from a waterworks. Cross the stile to the right of a large gate and now walk ahead from the stile, crossing a stream. Climb up a couple of steps to follow a narrow path that leads gradually uphill towards St Keverne village. At the main road, turn left and return to the village square.

WALK
17

DISTANCE
3.5
MILES

TIME
2
HOURS

MAP REF.
ORDNANCE SURVEY LANDRANGER 204
791
213

WALK GRADE
EASY

Warning: Parts of this route can be muddy.

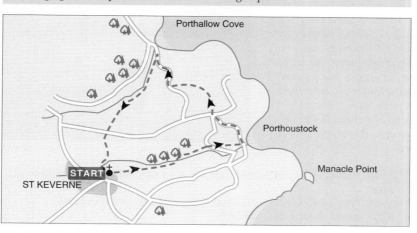

Porthallow Cove

Porthoustock

Manacle Point

START

ST KEVERNE

*The Gweek Inn, Gweek. MDN*

# RNAS CULDROSE PUBLIC VIEWPOINT AND GWEEK

*RNAS Culdrose, situated near Helston, is Europe's largest military helicopter base and home to the search and rescue squadrons that play such a vital role in ensuring the safety of mariners. The base, at times can be a hive of activity; a public viewing area, from where this walk commences, has been thoughtfully provided to allow enthusiasts to watch the aircraft. After following the perimeter of the base for a short distance, the route continues along field paths and quiet lanes to reach the village of Gweek. Situated at the head of the Helford River, the settlement grew as an important port, serving the surrounding tin mining area, but silting over a long period of time has ensured that most current waterside activity is mainly leisure orientated. The village is also home to one of Cornwall's most popular visitor attractions, the Gweek Seal Sanctuary.*

*Bridge, Gweek. MDN*

**REFRESHMENTS & TOILETS**
Toilets in car park, nearby café and shop also. Pub at Gweek (mid point).

**DIRECTIONS TO START**
The public viewpoint car park is signed from the B3293/A3083 roundabout south of Helston.

## WALK DIRECTIONS

Walk out of the car park and follow the road ahead (the café over the hedge to the left). Walk on to find a public footpath sign (also bridleway) on the left, adjacent to Rose-in-the Bush Park. Do not enter the park but instead continue ahead, following a wide track between high hedges. The track eventually bears right, away from the airbase boundary fence, following a grassy path between a fence and a hedge. Proceed through a slightly overgrown area before using a gate with a blue waymark. Continue on a wide track between hedges, descending to find a gate at the bottom. Pass through the gate and follow a boardwalk, path and footbridge alongside a stream to reach a road.

Turn right (ignore a bridleway signed on the right) and follow the road, walking uphill. Ignore a track signed as a footpath on the left and continue ahead to a point where the road starts to bear left. Here, turn right to take a broad unmade track signed as a bridleway. Where the broad track bears right downhill, continue

straight ahead. Pass houses on the right to reach a road.

Turn right and walk downhill, eventually reaching a T-junction. Turn left to visit Gweek (the village has a pub), otherwise turn right and follow the road. After crossing a road bridge, ignore the St Keverne road on the left and walk on (signed for The Lizard). Walk uphill (taking care as there is no pavement) and look for a public by-way sign on the left next to a track.

Take this track. Eventually bear right and pass above Higher Trevilgan Farm, the satellite dishes of the Goonhilly tracking station can be seen from near here. Follow the track past a further property on the left before passing through a gate and walking to the left of farm buildings. Gradually bear right, leaving the farm by a gate to follow a concrete driveway. This gains height before bearing left and proceeding to reach a tarmac road. Turn right to reach the main Gweek road (a fruit farm on the right sometimes advertises cream teas). Turn left and then take the next road on the right (signed for the viewing area), following the road back to the start point.

WALK
**18**

DISTANCE
**5**
MILES

TIME
**2.5**
HOURS

MAP REF.
ORDNANCE
SURVEY
LANDRANGER
203
**685**
**254**

WALK MODERATE GRADE

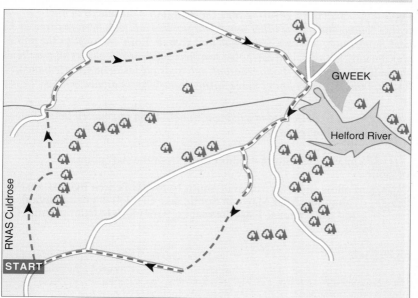

GWEEK

Helford River

RNAS Culdrose

START

*Warning: Parts of this route can be muddy.*

*Durgan. National Trust/Andrew Besley*

# DURGAN AND PORTHNAVAS CREEK

*Situated on the lush northern approach to Helford River, the quiet hamlet of Durgan is a place where time seems to stand still. Part of this may be due on the one hand to cottage ownership by the National Trust; the Trust protects from future development some sizeable land holdings hereabouts, ensuring that the area will continue to be the tranquil place it is today, and on the other hand, Durgan lies midway between two of Cornwall's most important gardens, Glendurgan and Trebah. Both are open to the public (see footnote for opening details), and are noted for their subtropical species in a valley setting. Trebah, well known for its rhododendrons and hydrangeas is in private hands, whilst Glendurgan, famous for its laurel maze dating from 1833, is owned by the National Trust.*

*This walk passes adjacent to both gardens, using a combination of country lanes and field paths to complete a 3.5 mile circuit.*

| | |
|---|---|
| **REFRESHMENTS & TOILETS** | In Mawnan Smith - a short drive from the start point. |
| **DIRECTIONS TO START** | Follow signs for Mawnan Smith from A39 Penryn by-pass near Falmouth. After Mawnan Smith, take first left (signed Durgan) and use National Trust Bosveal car park on right (start point). |

## WALK DIRECTIONS

Return to the main road and turn left, walking uphill. At the cross-roads, walk ahead on a no through road signed to Higher Penpoll. Descend with the road into the valley, passing houses. Ignore a public footpath signed next to a stile on the right and walk up the lane.

Immediately after a large house on the left (Barn Croft), take a track on the left and pass through a metal gate. As indicated by the waymark arrow, walk ahead keeping to the right-hand field boundary. Pass over the stile ahead (next to a gate) and walk on, still on the right, to pass through a gate. Proceed along the track towards a farm. Pass through two farm gates and then bear left down the driveway, which continues on to reach the road at Porthnavas Creek.

Turn left before turning right, signed as a public footpath, just to the left of a small parking area near the creek. Follow the tarmac lane uphill for approx. 60 yards to reach a narrow gap between posts on the left. Go through this gap and walk up the following field on a half right bearing towards a large house. Cross a stile to the left of the property and walk on to reach a tarmac lane. Turn right and follow the road past the entrance to the Budock Vean Hotel.

Continue on the road until reaching a bend; the road on the right marked to Helford Passage.

Here, walk straight ahead down a tarmac lane marked as a public bridleway. Where the track forks (farm on left), continue ahead. At the entrance to Trebah Gardens, again walk ahead, emerging into an open field. Walk adjacent to the left-hand boundary, ignoring a stile next to a gate passed on the left. Follow an old trackway which gradually descends, through a gate, continuing downhill to pass the entrance to Glendurgan Garden on the left.

At Durgan, follow the road past the Old Schoolhouse and then uphill, Helford River on your right. The road bears left to follow a series of stone posts joined by old chains. Halfway up this road, look for steps on the left. Take these and bear right to follow a woodland path running parallel with the road. This eventually returns to the start point car park.

DISTANCE
3.5
MILES

TIME
1.5
HOURS

MAP REF.
ORDNANCE
SURVEY
LANDRANGER
204
775
276

WALK
EASY
GRADE

*Warning: Parts of this route can be muddy.*

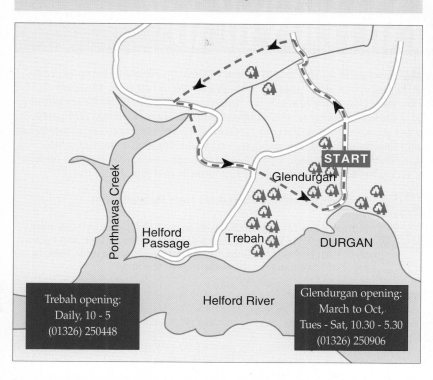

Porthnavas Creek

START

Glendurgan

Helford
Passage

Trebah

DURGAN

Helford River

Trebah opening:
Daily, 10 - 5
(01326) 250448

Glendurgan opening:
March to Oct,
Tues - Sat, 10.30 - 5.30
(01326) 250906

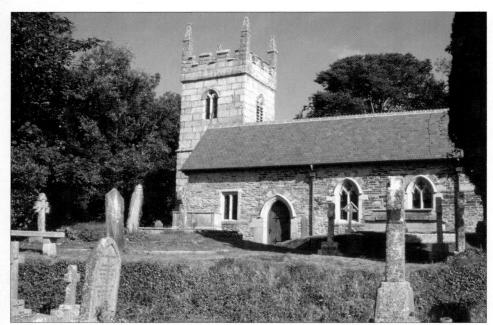

*Mawnan Church. MDN*

# MAWNAN CHURCH AND ROSEMULLION HEAD

*The route of this short walk starts from Mawnan Church, overlooking the entrance to the attractive Helford River. After passing through an area of tall trees, the route emerges onto the open coastpath to reach the National Trust property of Rosemullion Head. Like most Cornish headlands, this is suspected of being an Iron Age cliff castle; unlike most other promontories in the county, archaeological evidence is still somewhat sketchy. Equally unsubstantiated, are sightings off the headland of a large creature, some 20 feet long with a slender neck, small head and large hump. This Cornish Nessie, called locally Morgawr, has been seen several times in the last few years.*

**REFRESHMENTS & TOILETS**  In Mawnan Smith, a short drive from the start point.

**DIRECTIONS TO START**  Follow signs for Mawnan Smith from A39 Penryn by-pass near Falmouth. Bear left at the Red Lion pub in the village and take a right turn in front of Nansidwell Country House Hotel. Park in front of Mawnan Church at the end of the lane.

## WALK DIRECTIONS

Looking towards the lychgate of the church, take a path on the right to shortly pass over a stone stile. Advance down steps (public footpath sign for Durgan) and turn left to follow a woodland path which zigzags downhill. Follow the path east (i.e. the Helford River below right), climbing wooden steps and over a stile next to a National Trust sign for Mawnan Glebe. The coastal path now provides views across Falmouth Bay.

After crossing a stile, views across an open field extend towards Rosemullion Head. Cross two stiles and a boardwalk over a small stream before eventually crossing a stile indicating the start of the National Trust property of Rosemullion Head.

After rounding the headland, the coastpath gains height to pass over a stile next to a gate. Now keep to the higher path (adjacent to left-hand boundary) and pass over a large stone stile in the top left corner. Walk up the left side and cross a concrete stile. Follow a broad track, passing farm buildings and bearing right through a metal gate. Continue on the by now tarmac lane.

At the road, turn left and walk back to Mawnan Church and your car.

*Helford River. MDN*

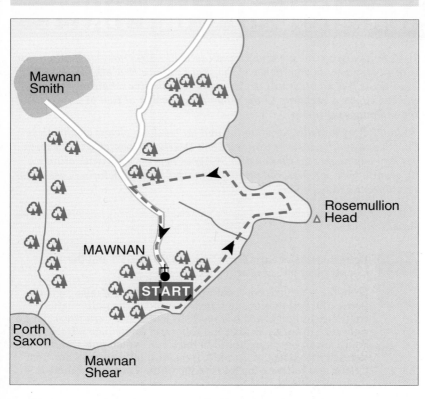

DISTANCE
**2**
MILES

TIME
**1**
HOUR

MAP REF.
ORDNANCE SURVEY LANDRANGER 204
**788**
**273**

WALK
**EASY**
GRADE

**Mawnan Smith**

**Rosemullion Head**

**MAWNAN**

**START**

**Porth Saxon**

**Mawnan Shear**

*Carn Brea Castle. MDN*

# A WALK AROUND CARN BREA

*Carn Brea Hill, with its distinctive monument and castle like structure, will be familiar to visitors to Cornwall given its dominance of the skyline above Redruth and Camborne. Carn Brea is like no other hill in Cornwall, it's massive whaleback shape and bracken covered slopes a backdrop to the urban development of two of Cornwall's most important and populous towns.*

*Carn Brea's 738 foot height provides for stunning and far reaching views; on cloudless days both the north and south coasts of Cornwall can clearly be seen with views west as far as St Ives Bay and further up the coast to St Agnes Beacon. This walk allows a chance to enjoy granite rock outcrops, old mining paths and even a Victorian castle that now houses a restaurant and tea-room!*

*Although graded easy, this walk is not recommended for young children in windy weather. Carn Brea is very exposed to westerly winds!*

**REFRESHMENTS & TOILETS**

Refreshments at Carn Brea Castle (01209 218357) and the Countryman pub at nearby Piece.

**DIRECTIONS TO START**

From the A30, take the Camborne junction (A3047, also signed Portreath). Follow signs to Camborne and at the traffic lights continue straight ahead (signed Four Lanes and Carn Brea). Take a right turn to cross a bridge and follow an immediate left (signed Four Lanes). Continue uphill to the Countryman pub and turn left to reach the village of Carnkie. Here, turn left (signed Carn Brea Castle) and follow a track to the top of the Carn where there is informal parking.

## WALK DIRECTIONS

Follow the track to the monument, the intricately carved rock formations passed on the way are all as a result of weathering. Pass the monument and follow a well-worn granite studded path that gradually loses height towards a further large outcrop of rocks. Shortly after these rocks, reach a path junction marked with a signpost detailing an outline of an engine house as well as blue and yellow arrows.

Turn right, following a path as it descends slightly. At a path junction, keep left and proceed downhill near an old boundary wall. At the bottom, bear left and continue ahead, ignoring path diversions on either side to reach a path just in front of a level sports playing field. As indicated by the waymark post, bear right to use a track between gorse bushes, telegraph poles running parallel just to the right.

The track eventually joins a wider one closer to the telegraph poles. Here, turn left and walk ahead to reach a further path junction and waymark post. Bear right on a track heading in the direction of the castle, passing underneath the telephone lines and gradually gaining height. Immediately after passing through a gap in an overgrown boundary wall, reach a path junction. Ignore the upward bearing path to the castle and follow the path bearing left, descending slightly. The track, much used by horses, passes beneath the telephone lines once again before descending to reach a wide unmade track and a large waymark post detailing the Great Flat Lode Trail.

Take the path marked with a blue arrow (i.e. with your back to the monument on Carn Brea, an effective right turn). This well-worn track leads ahead with Carn Brea Castle above to the right. It gradually gains height before passing under the telephone lines for the last time to reach a large path intersection. Here, ignore the sharp right path marked with a yellow arrow, taking the broader stony path up through the gorse (blue arrow). Pass close to a house on the left before proceeding on to reach the access road used on arrival. Now bear left on the road for a short distance before taking the path between a fence and a stone wall. The path continues ahead to reach the path junction used earlier in the walk. Turn right and follow the path back past the monument towards your car. Even if you don't desire refreshments, take a minute to walk on and see the outside of Carn Brea Castle, part of its structure appearing to be perched precariously on a large granite boulder..

WALK
21

DISTANCE
2.5
MILES

TIME
1.5
HOURS

MAP REF.
ORDNANCE SURVEY
LANDRANGER 203
685
408

WALK
EASY
GRADE

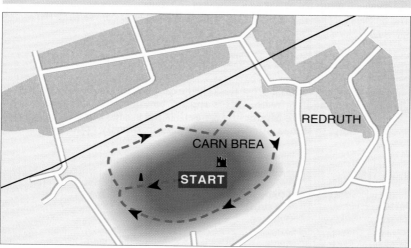

REDRUTH

CARN BREA

START

*Cliffs, Reskajeage. MDN*

# RESKAJEAGE DOWNS AND HELL'S MOUTH

*This route offers a pleasant circular walk in the countryside between Hayle and Portreath. A mixture of bridleway and field paths make up the main walking terrain with the coastal path encountered in the latter half of the walk. Views are across St Ives Bay towards the St Ives Island; visitors to this resort will know of course that the 'island' is no such thing!*

**REFRESHMENTS & TOILETS**

Refreshments in season available at Hell's Mouth.

**DIRECTIONS TO START**

Use the National Trust Reskajeage car park on the B3301 between Hayle and Portreath. This is approx. 1.5 miles from the refreshment cabin at Hell's Mouth (the car park is not signed but a stile and footpath sign is situated in the hedgerow directly opposite).

## WALK DIRECTIONS

Walk back to the entrance of the car park and cross the busy road to pass over a stile directly opposite, marked with a public footpath sign. Walk down the field keeping to the left-hand side - Carn Brea with its

monument visible ahead on the left. Go through a kissing gate and remain on the left, following a narrow track down hill between bushes. Pass through a gate to reach a tarmac road.

Turn left and follow the road to a

T-junction. Turn right (signed Camborne). After a short distance and shortly before the road crosses a bridge, bear right over the river to take a rough track. This soon narrows to provide shady though pleasant (but often very muddy) walking. Follow the track straight ahead for a distance of just under a mile before reaching a tarmac road via stepping stones.

Turn left and walk to where the road bears left over a bridge. Do not go over the bridge but instead bear right to take a rough track marked as a public footpath. At the top of the track, bear left in front of stone buildings and pass through a large gate, walking adjacent to the right-hand boundary. When the field boundary bears off right, continue in the same direction, uphill to reach two gates. Pass through the right-hand gate and then turn immediate right, walking up the side of the field. Pass over a stile ahead and turn right to follow the edge of the field before crossing a fairly overgrown stile in the corner to reach a tarmac road.

Turn left and shortly after passing a large barn on the left, cross the road right and through a gate. Walk down the field, keeping to the right (note views across the bay towards St Ives). Pass through a gate at the bottom and then continue downhill to find a gate in the bottom right corner. Cross a stream (muddy here again) and follow a fairly overgrown path to a track T-junction (stone building on left). Turn right and go through a gate and then left through another gate. Now turn right and walk along the bottom of the field. Proceed through a gate ahead and then turn immediate left, passing through a gate adjacent to the refreshments building at the top.

Cross the road to enjoy the Hell's Mouth viewpoint. Now bear right to follow the coastal path above tall cliffs through a gorse and heather covered landscape. The coastpath passes close to the road before continuing through three separate parking areas to return to the start point.

DISTANCE
4.5
MILES

TIME
2.5
HOURS

MAP REF.
ORDNANCE SURVEY LANDRANGER 203
626
432

WALK
EASY
GRADE

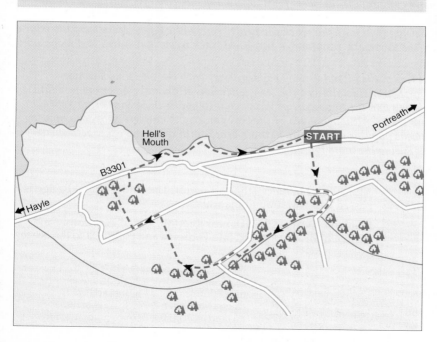

START

Portreath

Hell's Mouth

B3301

Hayle

*Warning: Parts of this route can be muddy.*

*Portreath. MDN*

# PORTREATH AND ILLOGAN WOODS

*This short walk can provide the basis for a lovely day out given its start point is the north coast beach resort of Portreath. The walk itself heads inland to explore Illogan Woods before using field paths to reach the Bridge Inn public house. From here the return route follows the Portreath Tramroad, a tree-lined track recently restored and reopened for public use.*

*The Tramroad linked the inland tin and copper mines with the one-time harbour facilities at Portreath. This allowed the transportation of tin and copper ore to South Wales for smelting and the importing of Welsh coal to power the engines that kept the mines free from water. Although much of the harbour area is now given over to housing, Portreath remains popular as a family bathing beach with cafes and other refreshment facilities open during the main holiday season.*

**REFRESHMENTS & TOILETS** — All facilities in Portreath (start point). The Bridge Inn at Bridge is passed half way around the walk.

**DIRECTIONS TO START** — From the A30, take the exit near Redruth, signed Porthtowan and Portreath (B3300). Proceed into Portreath and park next to the beach.

## WALK DIRECTIONS

Return to the main road from the beach car park and turn left, staying on the level with houses on either side. Where the road reaches a left hand bend, cross the road right and walk over a stone bridge. Bear left to pass under a small tunnel and walk along Glenfeadon Terrace. Walk on (now marked as Primrose Terrace) until reaching a sign indicating a weak bridge. Here, ignore the descending road on the left and take the route ahead marked as a dead end - on the right is a sign indicating Illogan Woods.

A tarmac track leads down to a path junction near the start of the woods. Keep left to pass through a gap in a wall and follow a woodland path; a stream is off to the right. Eventually cross a culvert to walk with the stream now on the left. Slowly gain a little height before passing granite posts (ignore a path leading right here). The path gradually leaves the woodland behind to reach a tarmac lane leading to a hotel. Bear left, heading uphill, before going right at the top to pass Illogan Primary School. At the T-junction in front of the school, turn left and at a further T-junction bear left once again.

After a short distance and immediately opposite Tangye Close, turn left to follow a public footpath between houses that leads down the side of a field. At the corner of the field, cross a stile and turn left, the field boundary now to your immediate left. Cross the stile at the end of this boundary and turn right, walking around the edge of the field. Cross a stile adjacent to a telegraph pole and proceed down the field, eventually descending to reach a small tarmac lane. Bear right and walk down to reach the Bridge Inn.

Walk on from the Bridge Inn to reach the main road. Turn left and walk on before crossing to take the first right - a dead end road signed for RAF Portreath. Walk uphill to reach a wooden stile on the left-hand side that leads to the recently reopened Portreath Tramroad. Although by no means tranquil (the road into Portreath runs just below), the Tramroad provides for a level return towards the coast on a route used extensively for the transportation of tin and copper in years gone by.

At the end of the Tramroad reach a tarmac lane. Turn right and walk to the rear of houses with long gardens before emerging on to the main road adjacent to the Portreath Arms public house. Follow Beach Road back to the car park.

WALK
23

DISTANCE
3
MILES

TIME
1.5
HOURS

MAP REF.
ORDNANCE SURVEY LANDRANGER 203
655
454

WALK
EASY
GRADE

*Warning: Parts of this route can be muddy.*

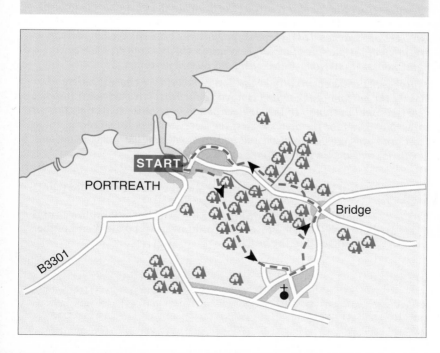

*Looking towards Chapel Porth. MDN*

# PORTHTOWAN AND CHAPEL PORTH

*This route commences from the coastal resort of Porthtowan (as **porth** means landing place and **towan** denotes sand dunes, a mental picture of the place is easily obtained) on the north coast, west of St Agnes. It is a landscape that has been changed by man over the last few centuries in the pursuit of metal ore, mainly tin and copper; there are several old engine houses, in various states of repair, passed en-route.*

*After heading inland, the walk eventually heads down the heather covered valley of Chapel Coombe. At the bottom of the valley is a National Trust car park with toilets and a small café (seasonal opening). In the eighteenth and nineteenth centuries, this site housed the processing works for the area's mines; the mine stack at Towanroath, arguably one of Cornwall's most attractive and photographed engine houses, was one such mine and can be clearly seen in the course of this walk.*

**REFRESHMENTS & TOILETS**  Both at Porthtowan (start point) and at Chapel Porth (mid point).

**DIRECTIONS TO START**  From the A30 near Redruth, take the exit signed Porthtowan and Portreath (B3300). Proceed to Porthtowan and park at end of the lane adjacent to the beach.

## WALK DIRECTIONS

With your back to the sea, follow the road on which you arrived, past shops and houses back to the T-junction. Turn left before taking the first road right (signed to Scorrier/Redruth/Truro). As you follow the road along the bottom of the valley, engine houses can be seen above you, a reminder of the rich tin and copper mining tradition of the area. Continue on the road until it starts to bear off to the right and then follow a track bearing left from the road, adjacent to a telegraph pole (if you cross a bridge near an engine house with a castellated stack, you have gone too far).

Follow the unmade track along a valley (higher ground on your left) and where the track forks, keep to the lower (i.e. right) path. Proceed past a water treatment works on the right before narrowing, through gorse, and over a stream. A shady path through light woodland now proceeds with the stream below left. Continue on between hedges before eventually reaching a tarmac road.

Turn left and cross a bridge before following the road for about half a mile. At a T-junction, cross to take a track ahead. Pass to the right of two cottages before crossing a stream and passing over a stile. Turn right and walk around the edge of the field before crossing a stile in the right-hand boundary and turning left, proceed uphill. Pass over a stile at the top to reach a road. Turn left and at the end of the road turn left again,

walking downhill. Shortly after passing a group of attractive cottages and just as the road begins to climb, bear right to take a wide track signed as a public footpath.

The track soon goes off to the right, but continue ahead as indicated by the sign, following a narrower track. The track soon emerges onto the side of an open valley, following an attractive route towards Chapel Porth. At a fork in the path, keep left and continue down the valley; the ruins of an engine house are off to the left. Stay with the main track until you reach a point where you can see the cove ahead; a broad, wide stony track (signed as the coastpath) climbs off to the left. Here, make a choice. If you want refreshments/toilets, continue ahead before rejoining the coastpath adjacent to the left-hand side of the cove. If not, bear left and walk gradually uphill. As the wide track starts to bear off to the left near the top, ignore paths heading inland and instead bear right, following the obvious coastpath. Follow this route back to Porthtowan and your car.

**WALK**
**24**

**DISTANCE**
**5.5**
**MILES**

**TIME**
**3**
**HOURS**

**MAP REF.**
ORDNANCE
SURVEY
LANDRANGER
203
**693**
**480**

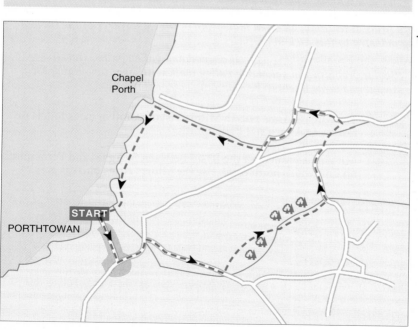

Chapel Porth

START

PORTHTOWAN

*Viaduct near Mithian. MDN*

# MITHIAN AND TREVELLAS COOMBE

*This route provides for a quiet country walk just a couple of miles from the busy resorts of St Agnes and Perranporth on Cornwall's north coast. Its start point, the sixteenth century Miners Arms at Mithian, gives an indication of the importance of the tin and copper mining industry to this area in centuries gone by.*

*The route involves some road walking as well as field and valley paths, Trevellas Coombe in particular providing an enjoyable valley walk with light woodland; the sounds of the stream and birds likely to be your only companions.*

**REFRESHMENTS & TOILETS**

The Miners Arms pub in Mithian (start point) or cafés/toilets in nearby St Agnes and Perranporth.

**DIRECTIONS TO START**

Mithian is located off the B3285 between St Agnes and Perranporth on Cornwall's north coast. Use the Miners Arms pub car park.

## WALK DIRECTIONS

From the Miners Arms, turn left to follow a lane downhill (signed for Perranporth). At the bottom of the hill, look for a public footpath sign on the left (signed Perrancoombe) and follow the path through light woodland. A stile provides access to a path across a meadow, a small stream off to the right. Walk ahead, following a route mid way down the meadow before crossing a

further stile adjacent to a wall. Continue in the same direction (farm buildings below right) before passing over a wall stile next to a large metal gate.

Turn right on the tarmac lane and after about 75 yards, bear left on a narrow lane (just before the sign for a ford). Follow this lane, passing Leycroft Holiday Village and Blowinghouse Mill (on the right) to reach a footpath sign on the left indicated for

Trevellas Post Office. Take this path which leads up a driveway to a house. As indicated by the sign, bear to the right of the house and ascend stone steps to take a narrow path between hedges. The path gains height through the gorse to reveal attractive rural views. Keep left at a clearing, the path levelling out to reach a tarmac lane. Walk on, the lane becoming a rougher track before bearing right (uphill) in front of a house with metal gates. At the top, turn left to reach the B3285. Turn left to follow the road before taking the first right, a small lane signed for Cross Coombe and Trevellas Porth. At the next junction, continue ahead (signed Cross Coombe), in front of you can be seen St Agnes village, dominated by the 628 ft high St Agnes Beacon.

Ignore the right turn to Cross Coombe and walk past Trevellas Manor Farm to reach a left hand bend

with an unmade lane proceeding directly ahead. Take the lane, passing a house on the left, and follow a small track down into Trevellas Coombe. Cross the stream via a concrete footbridge and bear left on a track uphill before taking the first left to use a track marked as a public footpath. This provides for a quiet walk through the wooded valley to reach the B3285 road. Cross the road to take a path immediately opposite. The path leads across the stream via a small wooden footbridge to reach a footpath sign for Wheal Butson. The path climbs a little before running along the edge of a field and just above a large house. On reaching the driveway to the house, bear left and walk under a bridge next to a large viaduct. At the end, turn left and walk to a T-junction before turning right. At a further T-junction, turn left and follow the road back into Mithian village.

WALK
25

DISTANCE
4.5
MILES

TIME
2.5
HOURS

MAP REF.
ORDNANCE
SURVEY
LANDRANGER
204
745
506

MODERATE
WALK GRADE

*Warning: Parts of this route can be muddy.*

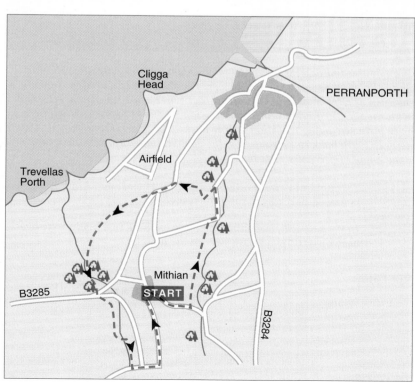

*Walking towards Cligga Head. MDN*

# PERRANPORTH, MITHIAN AND CLIGGA HEAD

*Perranporth is a popular holiday resort on the north coast and the starting point for this route. Famous for its three miles of golden sands (somewhat less at high tide), the town offers a wealth of refreshment opportunities that will be most welcome after this seven mile circular walk. The route follows country lanes before reaching Trevellas Coombe, home to a tin streaming tradition dating back 2,500 years. From here, it is an enjoyable coastpath walk back to Perranporth; the coastal landscape revealing man's pursuit of tin and copper over years gone by.*

**REFRESHMENTS & TOILETS**
Throughout Perranporth (start point). The Miners Arms at Mithian is passed half way around the route.

**DIRECTIONS TO START**
In Perranporth, use either the main car park just behind the beach or the overflow car park just up the hill.

## WALK DIRECTIONS

From either car park, return to the main street in Perranporth and turn right walking to the bottom of Liskey Hill (look for Lloyds Bank and gardens/boating lake). Take the road between the bank (on the left) and the boating lake, following the road towards Perrancombe. Walk past the church on the right and continue through Perrancombe for a distance of just over a mile. Where the road finally bears sharply uphill to the left, continue straight ahead, taking a road signed to Leycroft. Stay on the road, crossing a stream and ignoring the public footpath to Trevellas on the right. Pass Blowinghouse Mill on the left and continue on the road to reach a junction.

Bear right, walking slightly uphill before bearing left across a stile next to two large gates. Walk ahead, keeping to the right of a fence and farm buildings. Follow the path over a stile ahead and continue in the same direction as a line of telegraph poles. Cross a stile ahead and up a few steps to follow a narrow shady path that eventually reaches a tarmac road. Turn right, walking uphill before turning right at the top to pass the Miners Arms pub. Follow the road signed to St Agnes - in the distance can be seen St Agnes Beacon - and at a T-junction turn left (taking care, as this road can be busy).

Walk down the hill, ignoring a left turn to Silverwell. Immediately after the road passes over a bridge, take a public footpath on the right signed for Jericho Valley. This provides an attractive woodland walk, following a stream on the right. At a wide unmade track, bear right and then right again in front of a sign for Jericho Cottage to cross a stream via a footbridge. Now bear left (ignore footpath ahead to Trevellas) and follow the stream down the valley. Pass an engine house on the right to reach a tarmac road. Turn right and walk on the road until reaching a point where it bears sharp right. Here, continue ahead walking towards the sea.

After passing through a small parking area, bear right to follow the coastpath climbing, fairly steeply, away from the cove. After using steps, follow the coastpath on more level terrain above high cliffs. At one point the coastpath uses a tarmac way at the bottom of Perranporth Airfield, now used mainly for pleasure flights but a fighter station in World War Two. As you proceed further along the coast, holes in the cliffside reveal the extent to which this area was mined for tin and copper in the boom period of the nineteenth century. After passing through an, at times, barren coastal landscape, pass over the crest of a hill to see the three mile stretch of Perran Sands ahead. Use one of a variety of paths that follow the coastline here, eventually passing around Droskyn Point and through a gate close to the castellated Droskyn Castle, now converted into flats. Pass through the overflow car park to return to your car.

WALK
26

DISTANCE
7
MILES

TIME
3
HOURS

MAP REF.
ORDNANCE
SURVEY
LANDRANGER
204
756
544

WALK MODERATE GRADE

Warning: Parts of this route can be muddy.

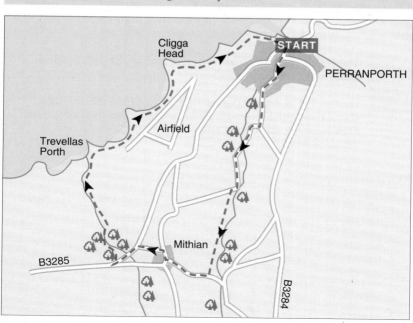

Cligga Head

START

PERRANPORTH

Airfield

Trevellas Porth

Mithian

B3285

B3284

Boscawen Park, Truro. MDN

# MALPAS, TRESILLIAN RIVER AND ST CLEMENT

*Situated just a short drive from the hustle and bustle of Truro, Cornwall's only city, this walk explores the quiet countryside adjacent to the Truro and Tresillian rivers. The Heron Inn, passed in the pretty riverside settlement of Malpas, is named after the bird that breeds in this area. The walk turns inland at St Clement, noted for its attractive twelfth century church and adjacent thatched cottages. A slate hung upper room over the church lych-gate, previously used as a schoolroom, completes the scene.*

**REFRESHMENTS & TOILETS**

The Heron Inn at Malpas. Toilets at Malpas, St Clement and Boscawen Park (start point).

**DIRECTIONS TO START**

On the A39 in Truro, take the Malpas exit from the Trafalgar roundabout. Just under a mile later, park adjacent to Boscawen Park (near the duck pond and children's playground next to Trennick Mill).

## WALK DIRECTIONS

Locate the tennis court complex in Boscawen Park and walk to its northern side (which offers a clear view up river to the cathedral). Proceed with the tennis courts on your immediate left, through a parking area, to find a riverside path. Follow this path alongside the river and pass sports fields. At the end of the path, turn right along the road and pass alongside Sunny Corner Quay. Steps at the end of the concrete quay lead to a pleasant woodland trail that runs parallel with the road towards Malpas. At its end, join the road and turn right, walking into Malpas village.

Continue past the Heron Inn on the left (toilets opposite) and on past a small quay area with moorings on the right. Ignore a public footpath signed up steps on the left and continue ahead on a tarmac road in front of houses. Near the end of a row of houses, bear right as indicated by the footpath sign before bearing left on a private road indicated with a footpath to St

Clement sign. This passes to the left of a house before using a kissing gate to take a woodland path.

Pass down steps and cross a stream via a small slate bridge. After crossing a further stream reach a point marked as Denas Road. This indicates the right turn to be taken now is a permissive path. The streamside path leads over a stile to follow a woodland path, at times with the aid of steps. Exit the woodland via a stile and keeping to the right-hand edge, pass over a ladder stile. Walk along the bottom of the field and over a further stile, following a woodland path just above the river. The track soon reaches the road at St Clement.

Turn left up the road. At a toilet block on the left, take the opportunity to divert right and see the lovely little church of St Clement, accessed via a small lychgate next to thatched cottages, before retracing your steps back to the road. Ignore the first public footpath on the left (next to the toilet block - signed Malpas) and continue up the road to find a bridleway next to St Clement Parish Hall. Turn left on this bridleway and

then take a path on the right shortly before a property called Druids Stitch.

Follow the obvious path (a little overgrown overhead) to pass through a gate at the top. Head across the field in a half-right direction, then walking up the right hand side boundary to find a track in the top right corner reached via a gate. At the tarmac lane bear left before turning immediately right (just to the right of a tarmac driveway). Proceed down the old green lane before you.

Ignore the public footpath signed on the left and continue downhill, the track gradually narrowing. Pass over a small stream via a footbridge and continue on the track up the other side. Emerge to pass adjacent to a tall wall on the left and walk past a gate on the left to reach a tarmac lane. Turn left and walk near a barn before proceeding straight ahead to leave the lane and pass through a gate into a field. Walk down the right-hand side before crossing a stile in the bottom right corner. Turn left to follow a track that leads beside houses down to the road. Turn left to return to your car.

DISTANCE
3.5
MILES

TIME
2
HOURS

MAP REF.
ORDNANCE SURVEY LANDRANGER 204
842
428

WALK EASY GRADE

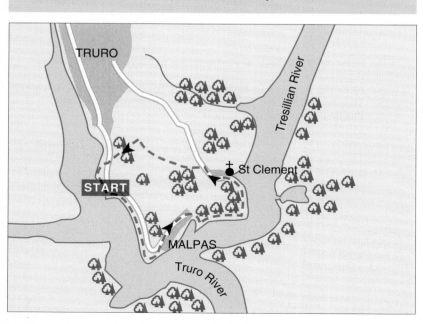

TRURO

Tresillian River

† St Clement

START

MALPAS

Truro River

Warning: Parts of this route can be muddy.

*Porthbean Beach. MDN*

# PORTHCURNICK BEACH, CURGURRELL AND ROSEVINE

*Portscatho, on the Roseland Peninsula, is an attractive small fishing village and coastal resort overlooking Gerrans Bay. Although tourism inevitably provides a means of employment here, the village fortunately is not exploited as are some of the more accessible settlements and is for this reason alone well worth a visit after completing this route.*

*The walk heads north along the coastpath from Portscatho's main beach at Porthcurnick. After enjoying views across Gerrans Bay, the route returns inland, using a quiet country lane before following a bridleway and field paths to complete this enjoyable and untaxing circular route.*

**REFRESHMENTS & TOILETS**
Seasonally available at Porthcurnick or all year in Portscatho.

**DIRECTIONS TO START**
From the A39 Probus by-pass east of Truro, take the A3078 (signed Tregony/St Mawes). Follow signs for Portscatho and to the Porthcurnick Beach car park.

## WALK DIRECTIONS

From the left-hand end of the car park (assuming you are facing the sea), pass through a gate and bear left on a grassy path signed to Porthcurnick Beach. A gate provides access to the coastpath before passing through a further gate and steps down to the beach. Cross the beach and proceed up the concrete lane on the other side of the beach before turning right through a gate to follow the coastpath again.

There are enjoyable sea views to the right towards Portscatho. Follow the coastpath

around a small headland (with a small stone building), views are now across Gerrans Bay to Nare Head. Pass through a gate and down steps, the attractive and secluded Porthbean Beach can be seen ahead. The coastpath passes around the edge of a field and across stiles before proceeding down steps onto Porthbean Beach.

Head left and after only a few yards, bear left away from the beach to follow a stepped path. Keep right at a path fork and walk on between hedges, ignoring a footpath on the left to cross a stile ahead. Walk over the field and stay with the coastpath to cross a series of stiles and footbridges before passing around a small hillock. Reach a waymark post adjacent to a small cove and turn left signed as a public footpath for Curgurrell.

Walk through a gate and proceed up a track. Shortly before a gate, bear left and cross a stile to take a narrow path that leads uphill to a track alongside a farmhouse. Walk on through a large white gate. Where the farm track/drive joins a tarmac road on a bend, continue uphill to eventually reach a T-junction.

Now turn right (taking care as this road can be busy) before crossing the road left to follow a tarmac road downhill (traffic light on left). Where the road bears right, leave the road to take a public bridleway signed on the left. Now walk straight ahead, ignoring side paths, the bridleway eventually reaching a road. Bear right and walk for about 25 yards before crossing the road left to pass over a stile. Proceed across the field and over a second stile. Cross a further field and stile in the same manner before crossing a third field adjacent to the left-hand

boundary. Cross the stile in the far-left corner and then proceed in the next field on a half-left bearing to find a tall stile on the left side. Now cross the field diagonally to the bottom left corner, just above the farm. Pass through a metal gate and walk down the left of the field. After a further metal gate, bear left and through another gate. Walk down past the barn to turn left in front of the farmhouse and follow a tarmac lane away from the farm.

Cross the road and take a stile opposite marked as a footpath to Rosevine. Cross the field ahead on a half right bearing and cross a stile on the far right. Now go a few yards left before descending to a stream, walking in the direction of the bungalow on the ridge. Cross over stepping stones and continue up to the bungalow. Pass over a stile in the boundary fence, a fenced path leads to a tarmac lane. Turn right and walk through the hamlet of Rosevine to reach Porthcurnick Beach once again. Retrace your earlier route across the beach and through gates, heading back uphill to your car.

## WALK 28

**DISTANCE**

**3.5 MILES**

**TIME**

**2 HOURS**

**MAP REF.**

ORDNANCE SURVEY LANDRANGER 204

**878 358**

WALK EASY GRADE

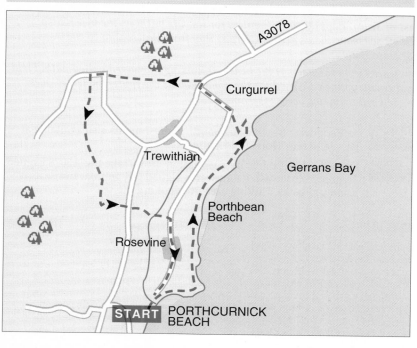

*Pendower Beach. MDN*

# PENDOWER BEACH AND TREWORLAS

*Pendower Beach, the start point for this route, is situated on the fertile Roseland Peninsula, east of Truro. Popular with families for its safe bathing, the beach also provides excellent seascape views across Gerrans Bay from Portscatho to the promontory of Nare Head.*

*The walk commences from the back of the beach, following a wooded valley path. Field paths and quiet country lanes are used for the remainder of the route; the latter part again provides rewarding views across Gerrans Bay.*

**REFRESHMENTS & TOILETS**  At Pendower Beach (start point). Refreshments also available at Polsue Manor Hotel (mid point).

**DIRECTIONS TO START**  From the A39 Probus by-pass east of Truro, take the A3078 (signed Tregony/St Mawes). Pendower is signed left approx. 1 mile after Ruanhighlanes. Parking area overlooking the sea.

## WALK DIRECTIONS

Walk down the lane past the Pendower Beach House Hotel. Near the hotel entrance, do not bear right to the beach but take a narrow track ahead that leads over a footbridge. Bear left and pass through a gap in the wall to walk through a parking area (toilets are up the tarmac lane a little on the right). Find a public bridleway signed from the top of the

car park that proceeds up the valley. The route leads through woodland before passing through a wooden gate to walk left on a tarmac lane past detached properties.

The public footpath continues in the far-left corner, crossing a footbridge before following a woodland path uphill. The path continues along the side of the valley before descending to cross a stile to reach a tarmac road. Turn left and walk uphill to reach a T-junction and the main road. Turn right (taking care as this road can be busy) and after approx. 60 yards, cross the road left to pass through a gate. Walk down the right side of the field. Where the boundary starts to bear left, go through the second of two gates on the right and walk down the field in the direction of the farmhouse.

Go through a gate and turn right, heading up a wide track. Pass Lambourne Farm on the left to reach a road. Turn left and walk downhill before proceeding uphill to go by Polsue Manor Hotel on the left. Shortly after the hotel, the road widens to provide a passing place for cars. Just as the road narrows, look for a public footpath sign on the left and proceed through the adjacent gate. Walk alongside the left-hand boundary before reaching a stile (near an entrance to the hotel). Cross the stile and follow a narrow track that leads over a stream and wooden stile.

Emerge into an open field and continue ahead, on the left, to reach a track. The track passes to the left of a farmhouse to reach a waymarked stile. Cross the stile and over the corner of the field, diagonally, before using a tall stone stile. Now walk with the hedge boundary on your right. Cross a stile next to a derelict farm building and walk to the field boundary at the top (left of a farm building). At the boundary, turn right and walk alongside the barn to reach a road.

Turn left and walk uphill into a small hamlet (Treworlas). Shortly after passing a large property on the right (the road also bearing left) take a public footpath signed to Pendower Beach on the right. Pass over a stile and walk across a field to reach the main road again. Cross ahead and pass up steps on the opposite side. Walk ahead, Gerrans Bay gradually coming into view before crossing a stile near two telegraph poles. Walk down the left of the field, crossing a stile ahead and continuing alongside the field boundary. Cross a stile on the left to follow a narrow track steeply downhill, reaching the lane to the beach used earlier. Turn right and walk uphill to your car.

DISTANCE
3
MILES

TIME
1.5
HOURS

MAP REF.
ORDNANCE SURVEY LANDRANGER 204
895 381

WALK MODERATE GRADE

*Warning: Parts of this route can be muddy.*

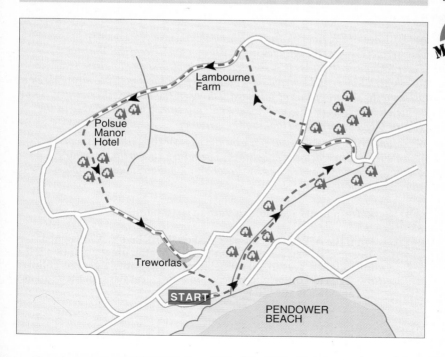

Lambourne Farm

Polsue Manor Hotel

Treworlas

START

PENDOWER BEACH

*Portloe. MDN*

# PORTLOE AND VERYAN BAY

*The small fishing village of Portloe, on the Roseland Peninsula, remains one of Cornwall's most attractive coastal villages, unspoilt by commercialism that has changed other attractive settlements. It is located at the end of a deep valley, reached only by narrow country lanes, and centred on a small cleft in the coastline allowing in a relatively small way the development of pilchard fishing in the nineteenth century. Some fishing is still carried out; locally caught lobster and crab sometimes available in the seventeenth century Lugger Hotel, overlooking the slipway.*

*The route heads inland from the small car park on the edge of the village, using farm paths and lanes to eventually reach the coastpath. The return to Portloe provides interesting sea views; a tearoom as well as the hotel and a pub provide welcome refreshments to complete your visit.*

**REFRESHMENTS & TOILETS**    Refreshments available in Portloe (start point).

**DIRECTIONS TO START**    From the A39 Probus by-pass east of Truro, take A3078 (signed Tregony/St Mawes). Stay with the A3078 after Tregony until a left turn (signed Veryan & Portloe) immediately after a garage. Follow the signs to Portloe and proceed to a small car park on the right at the entrance to the village.

## WALK DIRECTIONS

Return to the road and turn left, walking uphill. Pass a residential road on the right (a footpath sign on the left here should be ignored) and stay on the road to pass the driveway entrance with slate posts. Take the next right from this point through a kissing gate marked with a footpath sign. At the end of the wall by the house, bear half left across the field to pass over a stile next to a gate in the top left corner.

Follow a broad farm track. Through a gate and walk past a large barn on the right before bearing right to walk away from the farm on a concrete drive. Follow the drive left to reach a road. Turn right, walking past a right turn signed to Veryan Vineyard. Take the next right turn after this (near to where the road bears left downhill) and follow the road, indicated as a public bridleway.

At the end of the road, just before Morvah Cottage, bear right to follow a grassy track. Walk ahead before bearing right to reach a junction of paths with a three-finger waymark post. Turn right (coastpath signed to Portloe), initially descending before bearing right and eventually crossing adjacent footbridges. After a stile, the coastpath passes through an area of trees. A further stile indicates the route goes through the National Trust property of Tregenna.

Now simply follow the coastpath, narrow in places, passing through kissing gates on the return to Portloe. The path eventually passes adjacent to the old coastguard lookout post to provide the first views over Portloe Cove. Pass down steps next to a metal handrail and follow a path left in front of cottages that proceeds around to reach the main road. Turn left to visit the cove or take refreshments; turn right to walk uphill to return to the car park.

WALK
30

DISTANCE
3.5
MILES

TIME
2
HOURS

MAP REF.
ORDNANCE
SURVEY
LANDRANGER
204
938
397

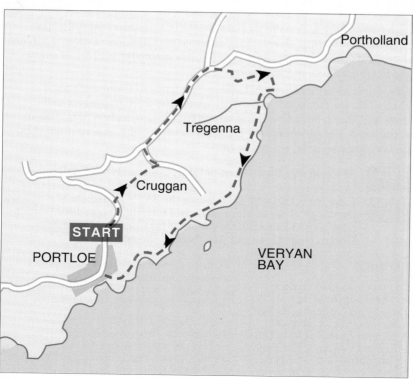

Portholland

Tregenna

Cruggan

START

PORTLOE

VERYAN BAY

*Caerhayes Beach. MDN*

# CAERHAYES BEACH AND DODMAN POINT

*Caerhayes Beach (sometimes referred to as Porthluney) is a popular family bathing location overlooking Veryan Bay. Overlooking the beach is Caerhayes Castle, a private residence that opens its gardens for a short time in early spring for visitors to enjoy view camellias, rhododendrons and magnolias.*

*Included in the route is an exploration of Dodman Point, one of Cornwall's most spectacular headlands. The Dodman's defensive capabilities were recognised and enhanced by Iron Age Man who built a massive earthwork fortification here. This is known as the 'Bulwark' and consisted of a tall bank of earth above a deep ditch. Also on the headland is a granite cross, erected in 1896.*

**REFRESHMENTS & TOILETS**

**At Caerhayes Beach (start point -refreshments seasonal).**

**DIRECTIONS TO START**

**From the A390 in St Austell take the B3273 signed for Mevagissey. Do not go as far as Mevagissey but turn right signed for Gorran (also signed Heligan). Follow signs for Caerhayes from near Gorran High Lanes and park behind the beach.**

## WALK DIRECTIONS

Return to the main road and turn right, passing in front of Caerhayes Castle gatehouse. Reach a kissing gate on the right with a footpath sign and proceed ahead across the field. After climbing a little, bear sharp right to cross a stile and follow the grassy coastpath, Caerhayes Beach below right. The coastpath climbs and passes over a stile on the right. Pass up steps in an area of trees before emerging to a viewpoint across Greeb Point to Dodman Point (also sometimes just referred to as The Dodman).

Cross a large wooden stile and continue on the coastpath. Two stiles and kissing gates are encountered before the path bears right downhill to pass over a footbridge. Pass into the National Trust property of Lambsowden

Cove, the coastpath now climbing behind the rocky headland of Greeb Point. The coastpath is easily followed here; pass over stiles and keep ahead towards Hemmick Beach, a sandy cove at the base of Dodman Point.

At Hemmick, join the road and bear right for a short distance to find a coastpath sign up the hill on the right. Take this and climb away from the cove, passing into a National Trust property signed The Dodman. The coastpath continues ahead before passing through a gate to reach a three finger waymark post. Ignore the left path to Penare (this passes along the bottom of the Bulwark, the man-made earthwork referred to in the introduction) and continue on the coastpath signed to Dodman Point. Cross a stile and walk out to the end of the headland. Note the enjoyable views from near the stone cross across Veryan Bay to Nare Head.

When you are ready to leave, walk back from the cross and past a small waymark post to reach a path junction. Leave the coastpath that proceeds ahead and bear left, following an inland path through the bracken. This path passes a small building near a trig point before continuing in the same direction. Use a kissing gate and follow a wide grassy path. This bears left to a path fork. Keep left and pass over a stile next to a gate, following a track between hedges. At the Bulwark path, bear right and stay on a wide track that bears left, signed to Penare, passing through two gates.

At the road at Penare, continue straight ahead, walking downhill. Continue on this road down to Hemmick Beach once again. Follow the road past the beach and walk uphill to find a public footpath to Boswinger on the right. Cross the adjacent stile and turn left, walking up the field on a half right bearing. Cross a stile and second field before passing a third stile to reach the road again. Turn right and follow the road uphill, passing a YHA in the hamlet of Boswinger to eventually reach a T-junction.

Turn left and follow this road for about half a mile to pass a sign for Tregavarras. Where the road bears right, take a footpath on the left signed to Caerhayes Beach. This shortly crosses a stile before proceeding in the direction of Caerhayes Castle. Head downhill to the road, turning left after the kissing gate to return to the beach car park.

WALK
**31**

DISTANCE
**6**
MILES

TIME
**3**
HOURS

MAP REF.
ORDNANCE SURVEY LANDRANGER 204
**973**
**413**

WALK TOUGH GRADE

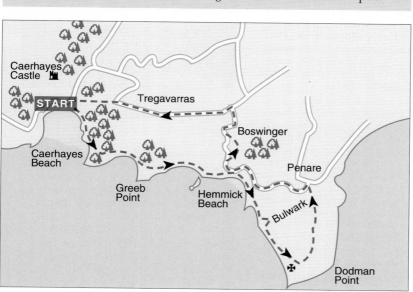

# MEVAGISSEY, GORRAN HAVEN AND PORTMELLON

*Mevagissey, an archetypal Cornish fishing village with a large harbour, draws large numbers of visitors throughout the year. The development of the harbour area loved by tourists today, was as a result of a prosperity brought by pilchards, the catch salted in large barrels on the quayside and exported in vast quantities to Mediterranean countries.*

*This enjoyable route heads inland from Mevagissey, using field and woodland paths, before reaching the small harbourside village of Gorran Haven. A stunning coastpath walk then returns via Chapel Point and Portmellon to Mevagissey once again, where there is a large choice of refreshment opportunities.*

**REFRESHMENTS & TOILETS**

In Mevagissey (start point) and at Gorran Churchtown, Gorran Haven and Portmellon.

**DIRECTIONS TO START**

From the A390 in St Austell, take the B3273 signed for Mevagissey. Park in the car and coach park on the left at the entrance to the village (if closed in winter, use one of several smaller car parks nearby).

## WALK DIRECTIONS

Turn left out of the car park heading towards Mevagissey harbour. At the end of the road, next to the Ship Inn, bear right to follow the road uphill, the harbour now on your left. Pass the Harbour Lights freehouse on the left and follow the road, views to the left are towards Chapel Point. Just as the road starts to descend towards Portmellon, take Penwarne Lane on the right (marked as a public footpath). Walk forward on an unmade track, proceeding directly ahead on the latter part between hedges to reach a road (a sign on the right indicates Higher Well Park).

Turn left down the road and after a short distance bear right signed for Penwarne Farm. Walk to the left of farm buildings (the main farmhouse is on the left) and pass through a metal gate on the right (footpath sign). Follow a track left, crossing a stile. A path now gradually passes around the side of a valley. Pass through a gap in the hedge boundary ahead and proceed in the same direction towards a further boundary hedge. After this one, follow a half-left path that gradually descends, through gorse, to reach and cross a small footbridge in the bottom left corner.

Cross through a gate and pass to the left of a house to reach a road. Turn left and walk

*Mevagissey. MDN*

through a gate, crossing a stone footbridge. Follow the road left and uphill for a short distance to find a gate on the right marked for West Bodrugan Wood Nature Reserve. Enter the reserve via a gate and walk on a woodland path. At a path fork, keep right. Cross a stile at the end of the wood and follow an obvious path ahead. At the far right corner of the field, the path starts to climb before crossing a stile in a fence.

Turn left and walk steeply uphill, the climb providing for far-reaching rural views. Cross over a stile at the top and walk on a half-right bearing. After another stile, cross the

68

next field in a similar direction. A further stile and field is crossed before reaching a lane. Turn left and follow the lane before bearing right through a gate to enter the churchyard. Walk around the church to reach the main road via steps. Turn left along the road, at first descending before then ascending - a tarmac path on the right should be used to avoid the road.

At the end of the path, ignore the footpath opposite to Carvinick and instead bear left on the road past the garage. Look for a public footpath on the right (a small stone building is on the left). Cross the stile and walk down the left of the field, continuing ahead over a stile on the left. Cross a small field and stile to reach a road. Turn right and follow the road downhill into Gorran Haven (keeping right at a road fork). Pass Gorran Haven car park on the left and proceed down towards the beach.

Turn left immediately in front of the cove, walking uphill (ignore the first footpath signed on the right). Turn right into Cliff Road (marked with a coastpath acorn), walking through a residential area. Walk uphill before turning right at a public footpath sign to Portmellon. Use the lane ahead and at its end, cross a stile to reach the coastpath. Cross left over a stile and head uphill and over another stile to walk on the fenced coastpath.

It is now a case of following the obvious coastpath back to Portmellon, ignoring inland paths but crossing stiles and footbridges when encountered. At Colona Beach near Chapel Point, with its distinctive whitewashed buildings, ignore the public footpath pointing inland and continue on the coastpath. Eventually emerge on a tarmac lane with Portmellon in sight. Turn right and walk between houses to reach the main road.

Turn right and pass around Portmellon Cove and up the hill. Pass the Harbour Lights freehouse once again, continuing downhill into Mevagissey. Explore the harbour and then turn back past the Ship Inn, walking up the road back to your car.

**WALK 32**

**DISTANCE**

**7 MILES**

**TIME**

**3.5 HOURS**

**MAP REF.**
ORDNANCE SURVEY LANDRANGER 204

**013 450**

WALK TOUGH GRADE

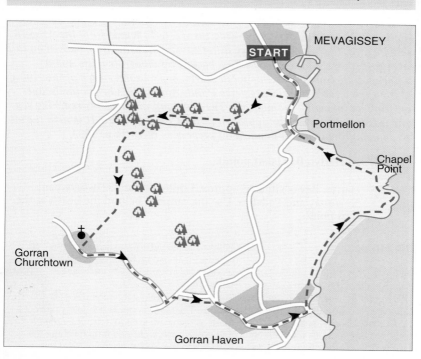

MEVAGISSEY

START

Portmellon

Chapel Point

Gorran Churchtown

Gorran Haven

69

*Trevose Head. MDN*

# HARLYN BAY AND TREVOSE HEAD

*The area explored by this walk, west of Padstow, is well known for its sandy beaches, popular with both families and surfers, exploiting the westerly winds from the Atlantic. Although closely located, the beaches are very different; Constantine Bay, backed by tall dunes and a large golf course, Mother Ivey's Bay, backed by moderate cliffs and a caravan park. Harlyn Bay, from where this walk starts, has a broad sweep of low-lying sand, sheltered from the westerlies by Cataclews Point. Amidst this beach landscape stands Trevose Head, an imposing promontory. The headland provides far-reaching sea views north towards Rumps Point, the approach to the Camel Estuary. It is also the site for a lighthouse, now automated, but manned by keepers as recently as 1993.*

**REFRESHMENTS & TOILETS**

At Harlyn Bay (start point).

**DIRECTIONS TO START**

Harlyn Bay is situated approx. 1 mile off the B3276 between Newquay and Padstow. Use the car park behind the beach as the start point.

## WALK DIRECTIONS

Walk back to the road and turn right (toilets are situated at the end of the car park on the left). Cross the road bridge and follow the road gradually uphill. Bear right opposite the Polmark Hotel to take Sandy Lane. Pass a couple of houses to take a public footpath on the left, a narrow track leading to a stile.

Follow the left side of the field before continuing ahead on an obvious path. A wooden stile next to a gate leads to a tarmac road.

Turn right and follow the road through Harlyn. The road proceeds between open fields, passing adjacent to a driving range and golf course. Continue until reaching the entrance to the clubhouse of Trevose Golf and Country Club. Here, turn right to follow a public footpath that goes through a kissing gate. Follow a narrow path that passes along the bottom of residential gardens. Ignore a waymarked path on the left and keep ahead, eventually passing through a further kissing gate to reach a path junction. Keep right, rounding the end of the golf course before passing down steps to get to the beach at Constantine Bay.

Turn right and walk along the top edge to find steps at the end of the beach. Follow a path that passes around Booby's Bay, a rocky cove popular with surfers. Stay with the coastpath as it starts to lead out towards Trevose Head, passing through a kissing gate. The path rises gradually. Cross a stile and bear right to follow coastpath waymarks, passing a deep chasm resulting from a collapsed sea cave. Pass over a further stile near the neck of a small promontory jutting out into the sea. Follow the coastpath up steps (lighthouse now in view). Bear left and cross the driveway before taking steps on the other side to walk above the lighthouse (metaphorically speaking of course!).

Stay on the level and well-used coastpath, enjoying the far reaching views across Mother Ivey's Bay and ahead towards Stepper Point and the Camel Estuary. As the coastpath starts the approach to Mother Ivey's Bay, walk alongside a boundary wall before crossing stiles adjacent to a lane to the lifeboat station. Walk on, passing through a gap in the wall to continue between the wall and a fence. Cross a stile at the bottom and bear left for a few yards before turning right over a stile marked for the coastpath. After a further stile, the lifeboat station comes into view behind you.

At Mother Ivey's Bay, the coastpath passes around a couple of cliffside properties, where a stile is then used to access a fenced path before eventually reaching a kissing gate next to the caravan park. Here, bear left, using steps to stay on the coastal path. Steps are used in parts on the coastpath to Cataclews Point, passing through a kissing gate. Cross a stile and walk in front of a large stone house and through an adjacent kissing gate. Continue on, following the waymarks and passing over two stiles before bearing left at a sign indicating that the coastpath now proceeds along the beach. Continue back along the beach to return to the start point car park.

DISTANCE

5

MILES

TIME

2.5

HOURS

MAP REF.
ORDNANCE SURVEY LANDRANGER 200

881

755

WALK EASY GRADE

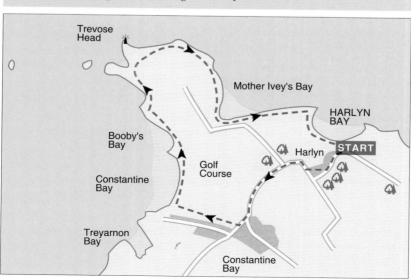

Trevose Head

Mother Ivey's Bay

HARLYN BAY

Booby's Bay

Harlyn

START

Constantine Bay

Golf Course

Treyarnon Bay

Constantine Bay

# LITTLE PETHERICK CREEK AND THE CAMEL TRAIL

This enjoyable route explores tidal creeks at Little Petherick near Wadebridge. The landscape is of small woods and meadows, bordered by arable and pastoral agricultural fields; the early part of the walk includes part of the Saints' Way pilgrim route between Padstow and Fowey. The Camel Trail, with its glorious views across the tidal estuary of the River Camel is also encountered.

*As this walk passes along a tidal creek, it is advisable to complete the walk at least 1 hour away from high tide.*

**REFRESHMENTS & TOILETS**

Refreshments available in season at Dennis Cove Camping Park, adjacent to the Camel Trail (mid point on walk).

**DIRECTIONS TO START**

Little Petherick can be found on the A389 between Padstow and Wadebridge. There is a small village car park situated adjacent to the river bridge.

## WALK DIRECTIONS

Turn right out of the car park following a road along by holiday chalets. At the end of the driveway, look for a waymarked footpath just to the left of a detached garage (note the stylised black cross on the waymark - an indication you are walking on the Saints' Way - a pilgrim route between Padstow and Fowey). A narrow path climbs through the trees above the creek. Cross a stile and use steps, following the woodland path before eventually reaching a stile to emerge into an open field.

*Camel Estuary from Dennis Hill Monument. MDN*

Proceed ahead, walking alongside a hedge/wall. When this bears left, follow a short path ahead to a waymark post indicating a right turn for a track descending between trees. Bear left at the bottom and cross a stile and two boardwalks. After a stile, follow a track uphill, keeping to the right at the top and enjoying the views towards the monument on Dennis Hill - a future destination. Cross stiles and fields, Little Petherick Creek below right, before following the direction of a waymark indicating a right then left turn down the side of a field. Descend on a stepped path to reach and cross a footbridge and adjacent stile.

Bear right, following the edge of the creek and proceeding uphill into a field. Follow the waymark direction, climbing across the field to reach a stile. Walk up the hill, keeping to the right side before crossing a stile top right to

reach a field with extensive views. It is worth taking a five-minute detour here to reach the monument viewpoint, accessed via the metal gate on the right (there is also a covered shelter here if the weather has changed!).

After the monument, walk downhill keeping to the left to pass through a metal gate. Descend and bear left before turning right down a tarmac lane. Walk ahead before turning right (public footpath sign) and passing adjacent to a boating lake to reach the Camel Trail via steps. If you want to go to Padstow, turn left (a ten minute walk), otherwise turn right and follow the trail, taking care to avoid the cyclists.

Cross the old railway bridge and then walk for just under a mile before passing through a railway cutting and over a small bridge. Now turn right off the trail, descending steps and taking an unmade track that leads off to the right. This passes Lower Halwyn before climbing on a now tarmac lane and bearing right to eventually reach a T-junction.

Turn right and walk along the road past a left turn (signed St Issey) and proceed on a no through road (signed Tregonce). Stay on the road as it descends, passing detached properties on the left. Where the road bears to the right (there is a barn on the right), bear left down a track towards the creek. Before descending to reach the creek, bear left through a gate (way sign on the left in the field) and follow a path diagonally downhill. Cross the stile and footbridge and turn left up a lane.

Walk for a short distance before turning right through a gate (marked with "Benuick") signed as a public footpath to Sea Mills. After just a few yards on the driveway, bear left and over a stile, turning right to walk along the edge of the field. Cross two stiles and two fields, continuing along the bottom edge before bearing right

at the end of the boundary and crossing a stile to walk between high hedges close to a garden. Bear left and follow a wide track adjacent to the creek. At a long property with built-in garages, bear right to follow a creek-side public footpath.

Round a small slate headland and stay creekside, the path eventually leaving the foreshore to climb a few steps and cross a stile. Now bear right along the bottom of the field, soon crossing two further stiles. Continue along the field bottom and over a stile before bearing right to cross a footbridge and stile - the holiday accommodation passed near the start of the walk visible across the creek. Further stiles and a footbridge are traversed before using a broad track that leads past a water treatment plant on the left. Continue on the by now concrete lane before walking through a kissing gate and along a driveway to reach the main road. Turn right and cross the bridge, turning right to return to the car park.

WALK
34

DISTANCE
6.5
MILES

TIME
3.5
HOURS

MAP REF.
ORDNANCE
SURVEY
LANDRANGER
200
917
723

WALK
MODERATE
GRADE

*Warning: Parts of this route can be muddy.*

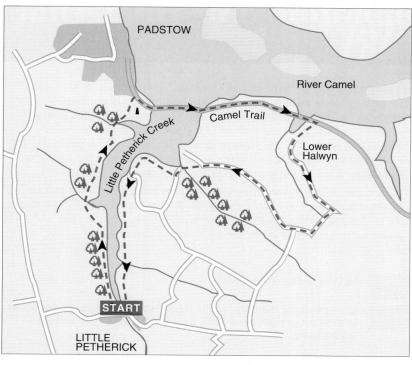

PADSTOW

River Camel

Little Petherick Creek

Camel Trail

Lower Halwyn

START

LITTLE PETHERICK

73

*Camel Trail, Wadebridge. MDN*

# WADEBRIDGE AND THE CAMEL ESTUARY

*This walk uses part of the Camel Trail, one of Cornwall's premier outdoor attractions. The trail is based on the old Bodmin to Padstow railway line, its conversion from track bed to recreational route undertaken by Cornwall County Council in 1980. The total length of the trail is 17 miles with the most popular section, part of which is covered at the start of this walk, the six miles between Wadebridge and Padstow. This walk will serve as an introduction to the trail and make you want to come back and hire a cycle to see the rest of the route.*

*Like the trail, this walk enjoys far-reaching views across the River Camel and its tidal estuary. A short lane leads to a field path providing the return route. The final part of the walk is through the residential area of Wadebridge, allowing the opportunity to seek refreshments or enjoy the ambience of this pleasant market town.*

**REFRESHMENTS & TOILETS**

In Wadebridge (start point).

**DIRECTIONS TO START**

Use one of the many car parks signed in Wadebridge and proceed to the start of the Camel Trail, near Bridge Bike Hire and the Lidl supermarket.

## WALK DIRECTIONS

Proceed ahead on the Camel Trail, walking towards Wadebridge by-pass flyover with the River Camel on your right. Take care, as this part of the route is popular with cyclists using the trail to Padstow. Walk under the flyover and pass the water works on the left, the trail now narrowing slightly.

Continue for a further mile or so to find a bird hide, overlooking the estuary on the right. Shortly after this, take a narrow track on the right (marked for Tregunna) and gain height adjacent to the trail.

Bear left over a bridge and follow a tarmac lane uphill. Stay on the road passing Tredale Farm before taking an unmade track on the left, immediately after Tregunna Farm (public footpath sign for Trevanson). Continue ahead (Tredale Cottage on the right) following an overgrown path between trees that descends (passing under a fallen tree) to cross a small stream via step stones. Pass over two stiles to emerge into an open field.

Bear right across the field, ignoring two gates on the right (the second leading to Roskear Farm). Pass through the third gate in the top field boundary and then immediate left to follow a shady track. At its end, pass through the gate ahead and cross the field on a slightly left bearing, enjoying rural views. Cross a double stile ahead and proceed on in the same direction to pass over a further stile, near a large barn.

Walk on with the barn off to the left to pass through a small metal gate, down concrete steps and then on through a wooden gate (not the metal gate on the left next to buildings). Take a half-left bearing and cross a stile next to some trees. After an adjacent stile, cross the field ahead and use a stile in a wire fence (near a telegraph pole). Now bear half right towards trees to find a fairly well hidden stone footbridge. Walk up the field adjacent to a stone wall and tree boundary. At the top, pass over two stiles just to the left of a bungalow and walk on to a tarmac road.

Walk straight ahead, between houses, and take the second road on the left (opposite "Longhayes"). The road bears to the right and over the Wadebridge by-pass before continuing straight ahead through a quiet residential area. At the main road, bear left down the hill. At the roundabout next to Goldsworthy Way, continue ahead for Wadebridge refreshments or bear left if you have parked near the start of the Camel Trail.

WALK
35

DISTANCE
4
MILES

TIME
2
HOURS

MAP REF.
ORDNANCE
SURVEY
LANDRANGER
200
988
727

WALK GRADE MODERATE

River Camel

A39

Camel Trail

WADEBRIDGE

START

*Port Quin Cove. MDN*

# PORT QUIN AND PORT ISAAC

*The tiny settlement of Port Quin, sheltering at the head of a rocky inlet on the north coast, is now little more than a few cottages, some of which are owned by the National Trust. However, in its 'heyday' during the mid nineteenth century, the community supported nearly 100 people, primarily involved in pilchard fishing, agriculture and small-scale shipping of goods. The pilchard harvest was concentrated in the latter half of the year and involved the whole village salting and pressing the pilchards. Although there was some local consumption, the catch was largely exported to Italy and other Mediterranean countries. The collapse of the population here is usually explained in a legend relating to the menfolk of the village being wiped out whilst at sea in a terrible storm. More likely however is a failure of the pilchards to arrive one season forcing the local inhabitants to move elsewhere.*

*This tough walk heads inland towards the picturesque fishing village of Port Isaac before following the undulating coastpath back to Port Quin. On the approach to the inlet can be seen a Victorian folly on Doyden Point, used in the filming of the popular seventies drama* **Poldark.**

**REFRESHMENTS & TOILETS** — In Port Isaac only (short diversion from main route).

**DIRECTIONS TO START** — Port Quin is signed from the B3314 between Wadebridge and Delabole. Use the small National Trust car park situated in the hamlet.

## WALK DIRECTIONS

Turn right out of the car park and walk on a tarmac road. Where the road bears off to the right, take a public footpath on the left signed to Port Isaac. Climb over a stile next to a gate, an obvious and well-used path proceeds ahead up the valley. After passing a field boundary on the left, a wide track bears uphill to the left towards two gates in the boundary ahead. Cross the stile between the two gates and walk on adjacent to the right-hand side. Use a further stile and right hand field boundary before passing over another stile (next to large metal gates). Stay on the right side to cross a further stile to the left of two gates.

Now bear left, following the edge of the field around to the right and crossing a stile in the left hedge. A narrow path leads down into the valley to cross a stream via a footbridge. Continue straight ahead, walking uphill on the right before bearing slightly left to pass a coastguard practice post (used when the Breeches Buoy Rocket was the main method of firing a rescue line from land to stranded vessels). Go over the stile in the hedge ahead, the

fishing cove of Port Isaac now in view. Keep to the left, a narrow path under a canopy of small trees leads over a stile before descending to reach a track that leads down into Port Isaac.

Bear right for the village and refreshments, otherwise turn left and follow a signed track on the right just before B&B accommodation. The coastpath climbs, up steps that provide lovely views back to Port Isaac. The coastpath passes around Lobber Point to reach the inlet of Pine Haven, an excellent picnic place or summer paddling spot. Cross the stile and small stream to climb away from the inlet. It is now a matter of following the obvious coastpath back to Port Quin. After passing a deep chasm, proceed around Varley Head, crossing two stiles quite close to each other. The undulating route eventually passes around Kellan Head - on the approach to Port Quin, notice the square building on the headland opposite, this is Doyden Folly (see introduction).

The coastpath returns to Port Quin via a stile and slate steps, passing between stone buildings to reach the cove.

DISTANCE
**4.5**
MILES

TIME
**2.5**
HOURS

MAP REF.
ORDNANCE
SURVEY
LANDRANGER
200
**972**
**805**

WALK
TOUGH
GRADE

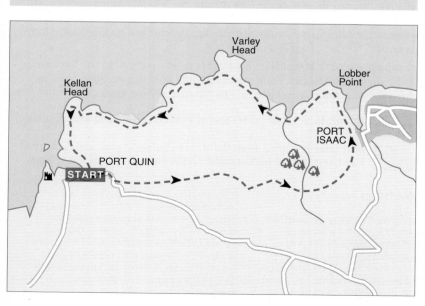

*Port Isaac. MDN*

# PORT ISAAC AND PORT GAVERNE

*Like Polperro on the south coast, Port Isaac is the epitome of a Cornish fishing village with narrow whitewashed cottages built above a small working harbour. The village has tortuous narrow streets and although popular with visitors, retains an essentially Cornish atmosphere centred around a harbour which has supported a fishing tradition since medieval times; its sturdy pier protecting it from the hostile waters of the north Cornish coast. The harbour was also used for the export of Delabole slate, seen on all houses of any age in the village, before the railway age determined a more cost-effective method of transport.*

*From the main village car park above Port Isaac, this walk descends to the harbour before following valley paths inland. Field and woodland paths complete a circular route via Port Gaverne, a tiny fishing cove just to the east of Port Isaac.*

**REFRESHMENTS & TOILETS**   In Port Isaac (start point) and at Port Gaverne (near end of walk).

**DIRECTIONS TO START**   Port Isaac is signed from the B3314 Wadebridge to Delabole road. Use the main car park located on the eastern side of the village.

### WALK DIRECTIONS

Leave the car park following the coastline (the sea to your right) on a wide track towards Port Isaac village. Follow coast path directions that guide you to a tarmac lane down into the village. Pass around the harbour and the old lifeboat station, following the road uphill out of the village

(Church Hill). Pass the telephone box to find a public footpath sign (to Trewetha) on the left next to a small cottage. Take the narrow valley footpath, passing through a metal gate and alongside a water treatment works. Pass through a wooden gate and continue ahead, following a tarmac lane to the right of a farm. Look for a gate (waymarked) on the left, just a short distance from the farm and follow a valley path again. At a junction of paths with a large waymark post, continue ahead (signed Tresungers). Pass over a stone stile and walk through a small area of trees to reach a path fork. Bear right, gaining a little height, before passing through a gate in a small area of woodland. Emerge into open valley once more. Where the valley path begins to bear off to the right, look for a small footbridge and stile on the left.

Immediately after the stile, bear right and walk ahead. Pass over a stile and continue in the same direction, climbing gradually out of the valley. Pass through a hedge gap and walk on a slightly left bearing towards a gate. Pass through two further gates and bear right in front of the farm (note castellated roof). Where the driveway bears off to the right (on the left is a barn), proceed through a large gate ahead and then turn immediately left. Walk up the side of the field and over a stone stile. Walk ahead and over a second stile, proceeding over the next field on a half right bearing to pass through a

gate next to a telegraph pole. From here, walk across the field following the line of the telegraph wires to take a further gate and field. Pass through a final gate to reach the B3267 road.

Cross the road and turn left to walk past a large detached house. Continue on to find a public footpath sign and stile in the hedge on the right. Walk down the left-hand side of the field and past a stile and gate on the left. Continue downhill to reach a waymark post indicating a right bearing path that follows a circular direction before passing between trees to cross a stile ahead in a wire fence. Walk on across the field, gradually descending and bearing left to the corner of the field (quite thickly overgrown with blackberry bushes etc). Follow a path left just above the stream in the valley bottom.

The path leads across a waymarked stile before winding its way back down the valley (crossing stiles on the way). On reaching houses, pass over a stile and walk ahead to reach the main road. Turn left and walk uphill, following the road back to the start point car park.

WALK
37

DISTANCE
4
MILES

TIME
2
HOURS

MAP REF.
ORDNANCE SURVEY LANDRANGER 200
998
811

WALK
EASY
GRADE

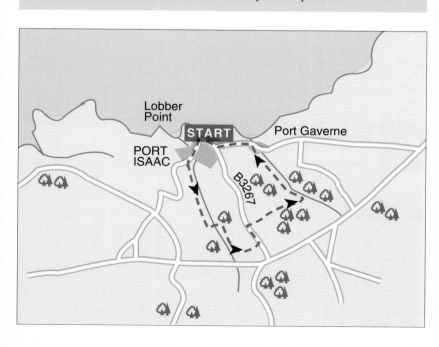

*Cyclists, Camel Trail. MDN*

# THE CAMEL TRAIL AT BODMIN

*This walk explores part of one of Cornwall's premier recreational routes, the Camel Trail. This was created on the track bed of the old Padstow to Bodmin railway line and provides a level, easily followed route popular with both cyclists and walkers. The trail here is much less busy than the Padstow to Wadebridge section and has a further advantage of a pub, the Borough Arms, located adjacent to the trail at the start/end of this circular route.*

*En-route the walk passes the massive walls of the former county prison, scene of many executions in times gone by. The gaol, (open most of the year from 10am - 01208 76292) is now a visitor attraction housing an exhibition as well as providing refreshments.*

**REFRESHMENTS & TOILETS**
The Borough Arms pub is at Dunmere (start point). Refreshments also available in season at Bodmin Gaol.

**DIRECTIONS TO START**
The Camel Trail car park adjacent to the Borough Arms pub can be found at Dunmere on the A389 near Bodmin.

## WALK DIRECTIONS

Walk to the bottom of the car park (signed Camel Trail) and follow the path down to reach the route of the old railway line. Bear right and walk under the bridge, now following the level trail ahead. Eventually pass under another bridge to reach the Scarlett's Well car park. Go out of the car park top left, turning right and crossing a road to

find a footpath (via a gate) on the opposite side. This proceeds ahead under trees. Continue on this path until passing in front of large stone walls (Bodmin Gaol) and reaching a road on the left, starting near an old stone cross.

Turn left up this road and walk past the entrance to Bodmin Gaol. Take the next road on the right, marked as a no through road

*Borough Arms, Dunmere. MDN*

DISTANCE
**3.5**
MILES

TIME
**1.5**
HOURS

MAP REF.
ORDNANCE
SURVEY
LANDRANGER
200
**047
675**

WALK
**EASY**
GRADE

next to a gate. Now leave the track and bear left to take a grassy path descending between trees. At a track T-junction, turn left and walk for 10 yards before turning right on a further grassy track that descends.

At a broad track sweeping sharp right, bear left at the apex of the bend to follow a track that leads between conifer trees. Pass over a stile next to a metal gate to reach a further woodland track. Bear left, it is not long before the River Camel (and a weir) comes into view below right. Continue on the obvious track ahead before eventually crossing a stile next to a gate. Turn left and pass adjacent to a metal rail next to a gate. Follow the broad level track, soon passing adjacent to a further metal rail. Proceed ahead, passing to the left of a detached property and along past a further gate. Carry on until you reach the road at Dunmere. Turn left and then cross the road, taking care, as this can be very busy. Find steps on the right-hand side which descend to reach the Camel Trail encountered at the beginning of the walk. Follow the path signed for the Borough Arms to return to your car.

opposite a cul-de-sac (Armchair Corner). Walk steeply uphill and follow this road, keeping straight ahead for approx. three-quarters of a mile, passing en-route a road on the left with a two storey detached barn opposite. The road ahead eventually descends to reach a junction of tracks (shortly after passing under electricity cables - a gate ahead gives rural valley views).

Turn left and follow a broad track through a gate and between hedges. The track bears to the right, crossing a stile next to a gate. The track then bears left, adjacent to open fields before descending to pass over a stile

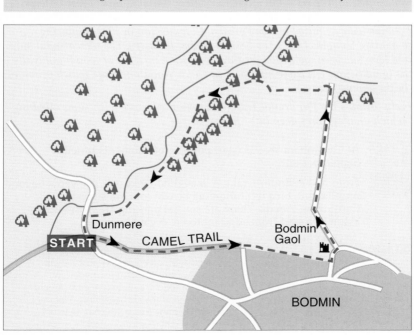

*Cardinham Woods. MDN*

# THE PANORAMA TRAIL IN CARDINHAM WOODS

*Cardinham Woods, just off the A38/A30 interchange near Bodmin, is a Forest Enterprise working woodland that also provides extensive recreational facilities. Now extending to 650 acres, the woods were acquired by the Forestry Commission in 1922 producing primarily high quality Douglas fir for the British timber industry. The recreational side of the woodland here has been well thought through with a mixture of woodland trails and cycle paths in addition to a cycle hire facility and a Woodland Café which provides refreshments in the summer season.*

*This route largely follows the Panorama Trail, a waymarked route with some climbing involved and which also explores deep into the forest.*

**REFRESHMENTS & TOILETS**
At Cardinham Woods (start point) - refreshments June to September only.

**DIRECTIONS TO START**
From A30 at Bodmin take A38 (signed Liskeard). 400 yards beyond roundabout, turn left following brown tourism signs to Cardinham Woods. There are several parking areas; the walk assumes a start from adjacent to the cycle hire centre.

## WALK DIRECTIONS

With your back to the cycle hire operation, walk straight ahead following a tarmac path past a large waymark post. Cross a stream via a stone bridge to reach a large waymark post detailing the walks available. Most of this route is on the Panorama Trail which is indicated with green ringed posts. Walk from the waymark through a wooden barrier and follow a wide forest track gently uphill, the play trail is below left. The track gradually climbs the incline before bearing sharp right. The track now slowly descends, following green posts, to reach an open area on the left with an overgrown rock face (possibly an old quarry) and a series of paths.

Ignore the minor paths and proceed onward using the same track that gradually bears left before continuing straight ahead. Further on the track bears right before continuing in a straight line again. Pass a bench on the right which provides a good vantage point across a wooded valley.

Continue on the waymarked track that starts to climb again. After a short climb which is steeper than so far experienced, note a green waymark post on the right indicating the route now leaves the main track. Follow a narrow path that gradually descends down the side of the hill before bearing right down steps and over a footbridge. Climb up steps on the opposite side before bearing right to follow a grassy path with the stream now below right. Walk on to find a path joining from the left. Here, bear sharp left and walk uphill to reach a bench and path junction.

From the bench take a sharp right, a waymarked path now gradually bearing left around the hillside, the views right indicate the height gained so far. The path eventually starts to bear right and descend downhill to reach an unmade track (a sign indicates you have just been walking on a bridleway).

Turn left and walk past picnic tables on the right before bearing right to walk over a road bridge and pass a large waymark post, marked with walking routes. Follow the road ahead over the stream, bearing right and walking with a stream below right. Ignore a path that descends from the left (marked with green waymarks but not required for this route) and proceed on, now following blue waymarks. The route runs parallel with the stream on the right before passing through a wooden barrier to reach a tarmac lane. Continue on, walking past Target Lodge on the left and Range Cottage on the right. The lane eventually leads back to the start point car park.

WALK
**39**

DISTANCE
**3.5**
MILES

TIME
**2**
HOURS

MAP REF.
ORDNANCE
SURVEY
LANDRANGER
200
**098**
**667**

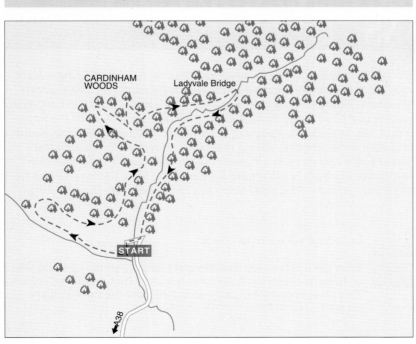

CARDINHAM WOODS

Ladyvale Bridge

START

A438

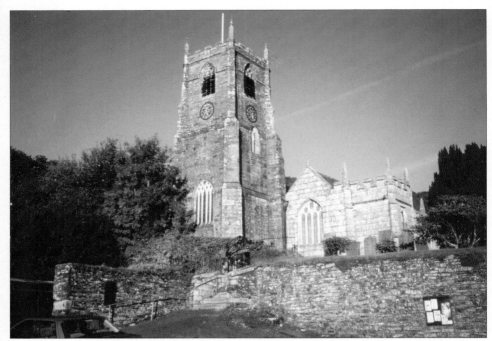
*St Neot Church. MDN*

# ST NEOT AND GOONZION DOWNS

*St Neot is a peaceful and well-kept village, nestling below the heights of Bodmin Moor. The village is sought out by visitors because of the church, famed for the quality of its fifteenth and sixteenth century stained glass windows which depict saints and angels as well as the Creation and Noah's Ark. St Neot himself is also represented; said to have been only four foot tall, he is shown ploughing with a team of stags. In the churchyard can be found a number of fine crosses, several of which are believed to be over 1,000 years old. Adjacent to the church, as in all good villages, is a friendly local pub, the London Inn. Just to the south of the village are the Carnglaze Slate Caverns, known to have been worked since medieval times and now open for guided tours (Easter to Sept 01579 320251).*

| | |
|---|---|
| **REFRESHMENTS & TOILETS** | In St Neot village (start point). |
| **DIRECTIONS TO START** | From the A38 between Bodmin and Liskeard, on the Liskeard side of Trago Mills, follow brown tourism signs for Carnglaze Caverns. Pass these to enter the village of St Neot. Use the signed village car park. |

## WALK DIRECTIONS

Walk out of the car park to the main road and turn left (the London Inn is reached by following the road right). Ignore Bush Hill signed on the left and follow Tripp Hill, passing cottages. Continue uphill, passing St Neot village sign to reach a point where a road bears off right, signed for Bolventor and Colliford Lake. Take the public footpath signed here on the left. Shortly afterwards, reach a path fork in front of a gate. As indicated by a blue waymark, bear right, following a path through bracken. At a further waymark, bear left, the church at St Neot now in view to the left. Reach a further waymark with arrows in both directions. Bear left, the path then bearing right in front of a gate, with views of the church, before eventually reaching a road.

Turn right, walking uphill, following the road with Goonzion Downs on the right. Eventually reach a junction of roads and take the first left (signed Polmenna). Follow this lane for about half a mile before it eventually bears left and starts to descend. As it starts

then to bear right, pass two gates on the left to find a third, newer gate, on the left. Pass through this gate (noting a detached stone barn on the left) and stay adjacent to the right-hand boundary, passing through a gate gap. Now swing broadly left to find a crossing over a boundary wall on the far left side. Walk steeply downhill to cross a stile and enter a wood. A steep woodland path descends to reach a track. Bear left and at a path fork shortly before a gate, bear sharp right, a stream now obvious below left. Walk downhill to pass to the side of a gate to reach an unmade lane.

Turn left and pass over a small stream before continuing ahead with open fields on the left. A curious looking tall chimney is also situated here. Pass Lampen Cottage on the left and Lampen Mill on the right, staying on the unmade track ahead as it passes closer to the stream. At a concrete drive for a farm, turn right and walk across a cattle grid, passing adjacent to bungalows. Walk ahead before eventually climbing up steps to return to the car park.

WALK
**40**

DISTANCE
**2.5**
MILES

TIME
**1**
HOUR

MAP REF.
ORDNANCE
SURVEY
LANDRANGER
201
**185**
**678**

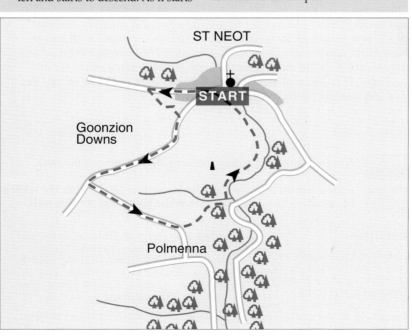

# RESTORMEL CASTLE AND LANHYDROCK HOUSE

*This walk explores the lush countryside and historic landscape near two of Cornwall's most historic properties, Restormel Castle and Lanhydrock House. The properties are separated by 500 years in their origin, but both are a graphic representation of the power bases within their respective centuries. Restormel Castle (01208 872687), now maintained by English Heritage, is located on a hilltop fortified since the Norman Conquest. It is the best preserved Mote-and-Bailey castle in Cornwall with a huge circular keep and battlements that can be walked around. The National Trust owned Lanhydrock House (01208 73320) dates from the seventeenth century and is set in 450 acres of parkland. It is regarded as perhaps the finest house in Cornwall and has 49 rooms and superb gardens for the visitor to explore.*

*The car park at Restormel Castle (the start point for this walk) is closed (along with the castle) November to March each year.*

**REFRESHMENTS & TOILETS**   None encountered within the immediate course of the walk.

**DIRECTIONS TO START**   Follow brown tourism signs for Restormel Castle from the A390 at Lostwithiel. The castle car park is the start point for this walk.

## WALK DIRECTIONS

Walk back to the car park entrance and follow the tarmac lane downhill. At the bottom, turn left through a metal gate to take a public footpath indicated through Restormel Farm. Follow the wide driveway as it bears to the right in front of a barn and proceeds between farm buildings and stables. Pass a large attractive farmhouse and walk on a tarmac lane, below right is the River Fowey. Cross a cattle grid and follow the lane ahead between open fields. Pass over a second cattle grid and on past a water treatment works on the right.

Continue to the end of the tarmac lane, pass through a gate and walk ahead across a field and through a wooden gate. Now follow a path that leads through bracken, bearing slightly right, before passing through a large gate to enter woodland. Bear left to follow a wide woodland track. At a soon reached fork, keep left and walk up towards a gate. Pass through the gate on the left and follow a broad track that proceeds into woodland. Continue until you reach an obvious track T-junction. Turn right, walking slightly uphill, the track bearing left to a stile and gate.

After the stile, continue ahead and pass through the smaller of two red gates. Walk ahead, passing a property on the right with attractive gardens. Continue on, bearing gradually left to reach a gate next to Lanhydrock House. Bear right and walk around the National Trust property to reach the crenellated gatehouse. Now turn right and follow a tarmac lane down an avenue of trees. Pass through a gate next to the lodge and continue to reach the main road.

Turn right and walk across the scenic Respryn Bridge, an ancient and important crossing point of the River Fowey. Ignore a kissing gate on the right and stay on the road, passing over the railway line and taking the first road on the right (signed Lostwithiel). It is now a case of following the road for about a mile and a half, gradually climbing to enjoy far-reaching rural views. Ignore the road on the left (signed Cardinham) and then take the next right, a road signed for the Duchy of Cornwall Nursery.

Shortly after the Nursery on the left, bear right down a track (opposite an impressive stone building with arched windows). The unmade track zigzags downhill to pass through a gate next to a stream. Continue directly ahead, over a railway bridge and a wide wooden bridge over the River Fowey. After the gate at the end of the bridge, bear left and walk in a right bearing direction next to a metal fence. After a further gate, walk up the concrete driveway and take the tarmac lane on the left (public footpath sign) through a gate. On reaching a road, turn right. In front of Restormel Farm, turn left and walk uphill, retracing the earlier route, back to your car.

DISTANCE

6
MILES

TIME
3
HOURS

MAP REF.
ORDNANCE SURVEY LANDRANGER 200

105
614

WALK MODERATE GRADE

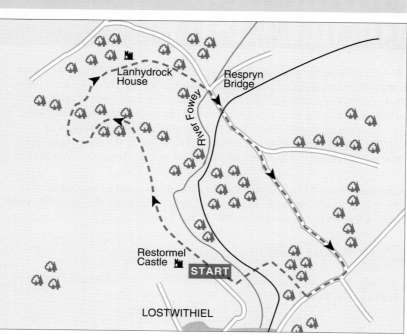

Lanhydrock House

Respryn Bridge

River Fowey

Restormel Castle

START

LOSTWITHIEL

*Restormel Castle. English Heritage/Alan Endacott*

# LOSTWITHIEL AND RESTORMEL CASTLE

*Situated on the lowest bridging point of the River Fowey, Lostwithiel has a rich and fascinating history that belies its unassuming appearance today. The town was once the administrative centre of Cornwall; the Motte-and-Bailey Restormel Castle, situated on a hilltop just to the north, is testament to the power base that was once established here. In early medieval times, Lostwithiel was an important port at the centre of a trade in tin; by the fifteenth century, the silting of the River Fowey from tin-streaming works upriver had meant that most of this trade had been lost to Fowey.*

*This short walk explores a little of the town before heading inland to reach the thirteenth century Restormel Castle. In the care of English Heritage, the castle is open between April and October (admission charged - 01208 872687).*

| **REFRESHMENTS & TOILETS** | Both at Lostwithiel (start point). |
|---|---|
| **DIRECTIONS TO START** | Lostwithiel is situated on the A390 east of St Austell. Use the signed car park near the information centre. |

## WALK DIRECTIONS

Walk back from the car park to the main A390. Turn left and then cross to take the road (Duke Street) leading uphill next to the Royal Talbot. Follow the road uphill to a T-junction and turn right, continuing past a school on the left. Shortly after a road on the left (opposite detached houses), turn left to use a public footpath that is accessed via a metal gate next to a driveway.

Follow the shady path, passing over a stile and then walking on a wide track between hedges. Cross a narrow stile and walk under a canopy of trees before descending, then over a stile to reach a tarmac road. Turn right and walk uphill, passing a road on the left. Take the next road on the right (Lostwithiel town sign). After only a few yards, leave the road and turn left through a gate (public footpath sign).

Keep ahead and pass over a ladder stile, walking in the same direction, Restormel Castle now coming into view among the trees on the right.

Near the end of the field boundary on the left, turn sharp right and cross a stile. Bear immediate left, walking along the top of the field to cross a tall ladder stile in the corner. Bear sharp right to walk downhill and pass through a metal gate, descending adjacent to the right-hand side of the field. Cross a stile to enter Restormel Castle car park.

Walk through the car park to the entrance in the right corner and follow a tarmac lane downhill to reach Restormel Farm. Turn right and follow the road along the side of the valley to Lostwithiel for a distance of about three-quarters of a mile. Over the hedge to the right can be seen Lostwithiel Golf and Country Club, whilst ahead, between the trees, can be seen the unusual octagonal spire of St Bartholomew's Church (used as a prison by Cromwell in the Civil War).

On reaching the main A390 in Lostwithiel, bear slightly left and cross the road to return to your car.

WALK
42

DISTANCE
2.5
MILES

TIME
1.5
HOURS

MAP REF.
ORDNANCE
SURVEY
LANDRANGER
200
105
600

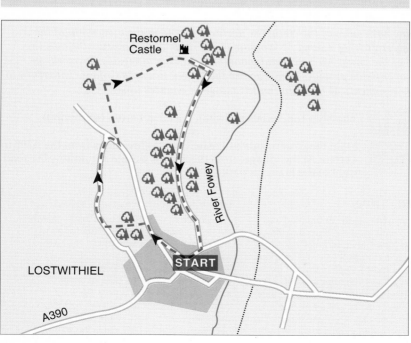

*Lerryn Creek. MDN*

# LERRYN AND CLIFF PILL

*Lerryn, situated on a tidal creek of the River Fowey estuary south east of Lostwithiel, is a quiet and picturesque village unchanged by its increasing discovery as a place from which enjoyable walks can be had. The sixteenth century bridge over the river is testament to the previous importance of the settlement; its tidal creek position utilised to serve the large farming community that was established on the fertile soils here. The name of the village pub, the Ship Inn, is derived from this river port role.*

*Woodlands line both sides of the creek; the northern side is in the ownership of the National Trust, stretching around St Winnow point - this walk however follows the southern side of the creek. After peaceful woodland walking alongside the creek, an inland climb over fields provides views across the Fowey towards Golant. The return to Lerryn (and refreshments at the Ship Inn!) is via quiet country lanes.*

| | |
|---|---|
| **REFRESHMENTS & TOILETS** | The Ship Inn, toilets and shop are all at Lerryn (start point). |
| **DIRECTIONS TO START** | From the eastern side of Lostwithiel, follow signs from the A390 to Lerryn. At the village, cross the narrow bridge and follow the road right to the main car park. |

## WALK DIRECTIONS

From the car park, return to the road and turn right to walk past the Ship Inn. Shortly after the left turn signed to Polperro, turn right adjacent to Bluebell Cottage (marked as a public footpath). Bear to the left of Woodleigh Cottage and after a small footbridge, follow a waymarked path that forks to the right. After just a few yards, turn left and then take an immediate right, following a path that climbs towards trees (opposite a property marked Tredour).

An attractive woodland path leads past the ruins of a stone fountain before following waymarks through the woods, the path ascending then descending to run just above the creek. At one point, the path descends out from the trees to cross stepping stones from where the walk continues adjacent to the creek before resuming a route just inside the tree line once again. Further on, cross the stepping stones over a small stream before continuing on a woodland path. Eventually cross a stile near a shed and proceed adjacent to a garden boundary. This then leads right before descending to pass near the creek once more - through the trees from here can be seen both St Winnow Point and the waterside village of Golant. Two stiles are encountered near the end of the woods before following a waymarked path alongside a driveway. A third stile leads to a tarmac lane.

Turn right and walk downhill to reach the tiny inlet of Cliff Pill. Shortly after a cottage here, take a public footpath on the left. This leads up a valley with a stream off to the left. Go through the metal gate at the top, walking a few yards ahead before turning right and climbing steeply uphill. Cross a stile in the boundary fence and walk directly ahead - Golant is now clearly in view. The path proceeds along the left-hand boundary to reach a step stile in the wall ahead. Turn left and walk up the side of the field before passing

through a gate ahead. Now walk with the field boundary on the right and after another gate reach a road.

Proceed ahead, following the road as it bears left and then right. Reach a stile on the left, marked with a public footpath sign, adjacent to Pennant Farm. Cross the stile and then bear left, then right, walking with the hedge on your left. Bear left through a gate at the bottom of the field and then bear right, keeping to the right-hand side and passing through a gate to reach a road.

*NB the remainder of the circular route is by country road. If you wish to avoid road walking you can turn left here and walk downhill to find the stile on the right used earlier, following the route back through the woods.* To follow the circular route, turn right on the road and then keep left at the first road fork. At a wider road junction, follow the road ahead (signed Lerryn), walking downhill and ignoring a small lane on the right shortly afterwards. Continue on the main road and walk past the pub back to Lerryn car park.

WALK
43

DISTANCE
3.5
MILES

TIME
2
HOURS

MAP REF.
ORDNANCE SURVEY LANDRANGER 200
140
571

WALK
EASY
GRADE

*Warning: Parts of this route can be muddy.*

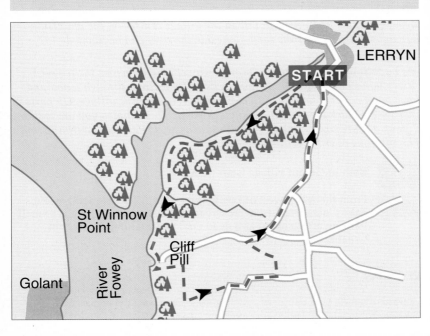

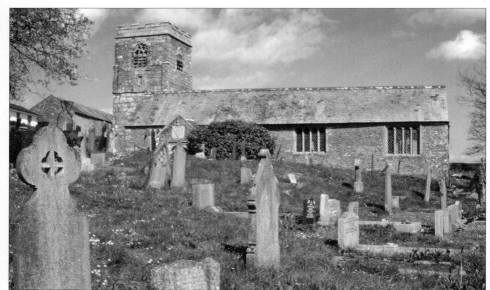

*St Sampson Church, Golant. MDN*

# GOLANT AND THE SAINTS' WAY

*Golant is one of those sleepy, tucked away sort of villages where the way of life appears relatively slow and the scenery spectacular. One gets a feeling, justified or not, that Golant is a place to where people move and ultimately stay; it is sufficiently off the beaten track not to be affected by large numbers of visitors but situated in one of the most scenic areas of south east Cornwall. Life in the village centres on the waterside, so much so that signs indicate that the road alongside the river can be flooded at high tides!*

*The walk starts by following a path which provides lovely views across the wooded slopes of the River Fowey estuary and nearby creeks. After a climb through woodland, the route follows quiet country lanes and field paths to return to the village. On parts of the walk you will see a black cross on the waymark posts. This denotes you are walking on the Saints' Way, a route connecting Cornwall's north coast (Padstow) with the south (Fowey) used by pilgrims over the centuries.*

| | |
|---|---|
| **REFRESHMENTS & TOILETS** | Both in Golant village (start point). |
| **DIRECTIONS TO START** | From the A390, west of Lostwithiel, take B3269 (signed Fowey). Take Golant road from crossroads at Castle Dore. There is a small parking area (signed as a dead end) overlooking the river in Golant. |

### WALK DIRECTIONS

Head back towards the main part of the village from the parking area, passing the toilet block. Take the first road left and walk uphill past the Fisherman's Arms pub. Bear left at the top and walk through a small parking area before following a tarmac lane.

At the end of the lane, take a narrow track indicated by a waymark post with a black stylised cross - this indicates the track is part of the route of the Saints' Way. The track provides stunning views down the River Fowey estuary and across to Penpoll Creek.

The path descends, bearing right, into a secluded wooded creek (Bodmin Pill). Cross the stream and bear right following the Saints' Way waymark. The path leads up through woodland. Leave the woodland by crossing two stiles fairly close together and follow a well-defined path across the field. The path leads over a further stile and follows a track alongside farm buildings. At the end of the track, do not follow the Saints' Way signs left; instead bear right along a lane signed to Lanherriot Farm.

Follow the lane as it descends and passes the entrance to the farm. Take a left bearing track (signed as a public footpath) that passes through a metal gate, following a fairly muddy route, descending between tree-lined hedges. At the bottom, pass through a gate and cross a brook before following the track uphill on the

opposite side. Bear left at the top to reach a tarmac lane.

Here, turn left (house and greenhouses on right) and walk ahead to reach a crossroads. Go straight across onto a narrow lane, where there are far-reaching rural views across the tops of the hedges. The lane descends before eventually reaching a public footpath sign and stile (Saints' Way symbol) on the right hand side. Cross the stile and head uphill to a further stile in the corner of the field. Walk up the left-hand side of the next field and go over a stile at the top. Cross a tarmac lane and further stile and follow a right bearing path across a field (marked with posts). Cross a further stile and field, the path then running alongside the left-hand field boundary before crossing a stile (or through the gate at the side) to reach a lane.

Turn left and walk past St Sampson Church, heading downhill back towards Golant. At the bottom of the hill, proceed ahead over the crossroads and pass the Post Office before bearing left and walking down past the Fisherman's Arms pub. At the bottom, turn right and return to your car.

DISTANCE
3.5
MILES

TIME
2
HOURS

MAP REF.
ORDNANCE
SURVEY
LANDRANGER
200
123
548

WALK
MODERATE
GRADE

Warning: Parts of this route can be muddy.

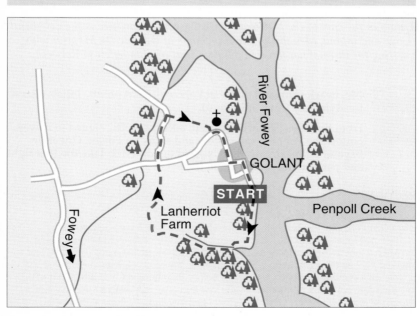

*Polkerris Beach. MDN*

# POLKERRIS, READYMONEY COVE AND GRIBBIN HEAD

*From the sheltered family bathing cove at Polkerris, with its waterside located Rashleigh Arms pub, the walk heads inland along part of the Saints' Way before using the evocatively named "Love Lane" to descend to Readymoney Cove. Adjacent to this small cove, probably named after the smugglers for whom payment was always required in "ready money", is the viewpoint of St Catherine's Castle. Watching over the entrance to the Fowey Estuary, the castle is in the care of English Heritage and can be freely explored as part of this walk. From here the route follows the coastal path around Gribbin Head, now in the care of the National Trust. En-route from here is the delightful Polridmouth Cove and inland, Menabilly, one time home of Daphne Du Maurier who used it as the setting for three of her novels including that of Manderley in* **Rebecca***.*

**REFRESHMENTS & TOILETS**

Inn, beach shop and toilets at Polkerris (start point). Toilets also at Readymoney Cove (midpoint).

**DIRECTIONS TO START**

From the A390 east of St Austell, take the A3082 signed to Fowey. Follow the Par one way system and signs for Fowey. One mile beyond Polmear, turn right, signed to Polkerris. Take the first right and park on the right hand side.

## WALK DIRECTIONS

Turn right out of the car park and walk down towards the beach at Polkerris. Just before the beach, turn left (signed toilets) and go past the toilet block to reach a fork in the path (next to a building marked 1912 on the right). Bear left, walking gradually uphill before bearing right next to a coastpath waymark post (acorn sign). Follow the obvious path that zigzags uphill through a small wood before emerging on a path next to an open field.

Turn left and follow a well-defined path across the middle of the field before passing through a gate to reach a road. Turn right and walk along the road before taking the first left just before Tregaminion Church. Walk down the lane and bear right before turning left in front of a large barn. Pass through a metal gate and go on through a further metal gate on the left. Now turn right and walk down a field before crossing a stile. The path goes along the edge of a field before crossing a small footbridge and proceeding uphill to a wooden gate. Continue up the right side of the field.

Cross two stiles before walking ahead between a wire fence and a hedge boundary. Pass over a slate stile and follow the path downhill, passing under a bridge and over a stile and stream. An obvious path now leads away, gradually climbing, before passing through a gate to reach a tarmac road. Turn right and walk past the first left turn before walking on to the next road on the left. Follow the road left to find Love Lane - a National Trust footpath - on the right. Take the lane and descend to reach Readymoney Cove (an information sign on the Saints' Way is near the bottom).

Proceed on to the beach at the cove and take wooden steps on the right. These lead to a stepped path through the woods to the viewpoint of St Catherine's Castle. Take a few minutes to follow the signed path and explore the castle remains.

From the castle, retrace your steps back to the St Catherine's Castle sign and turn left. Take the middle path away from the viewpoint. At a path T-junction, turn left and walk through a gate - you are now on the coastal path. Walk ahead with the sea now continually on your left - ahead can be seen the distinctive red and white striped daymark on Gribbin Head - this is your future destination. Follow the coastpath, crossing several stiles and passing around low cliffs before descending to a cove with a lake and house overlooking the sea - this is Polridmouth Cove, an attractive and tranquil place. From here there is an obvious path to the daymark, an outstanding viewpoint. Bear right from the daymark and pass through a gate. The coastpath is easily followed here; to your left are views across St Austell Bay towards Dodman Point and ahead can be seen the china clay works at Par. Pass over occasional stiles before eventually reaching the point used near the start of the walk that provides access to the zigzag path down through woodland to Polkerris. After following the woodland path, turn right walking back past the toilets to reach the road to the beach. Turn left for refreshments or to visit the cove, turn right to walk back up the hill to your car.

**DISTANCE**

**7**

**MILES**

**TIME**

**3**

**HOURS**

**MAP REF.**

ORDNANCE
SURVEY
LANDRANGER
200

**094
524**

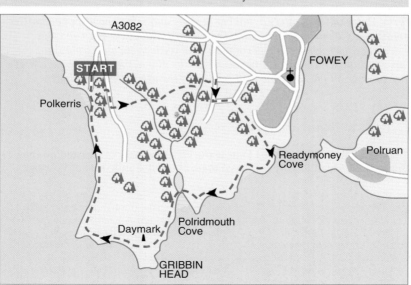

*Pont Pill. MDN*

# LANTIC BAY, POLRUAN AND PONT PILL

*This route arguably explores one of the most attractive parts of Cornwall, around Polruan near Fowey in southeast Cornwall. Although parts of this route were featured in a walk in the original **Classic Walks: Cornwall** book, the area offers so much for the visitor that any Cornwall walks title would be incomplete without it. The walk commences near the National Trust property of Pencarrow Head before passing around Lantic Bay, which has a small beach where you will often find yachts, moored on summer days. The coastpath walk to Polruan is easily followed and not particularly strenuous; the views up the Fowey estuary from Polruan are about as far-reaching and as good as it gets. Polruan itself offers a number of pubs and refreshment opportunities as well as a small quay where you can watch the estuary traffic; the tugs you can often see here are employed when tankers come to load with china clay from the works upstream. The walk then follows woodland paths above the attractive creek of Pont Pill before turning inland to allow exploration of the attractive church at Lanteglos.*

**REFRESHMENTS & TOILETS**  In Polruan (mid point).

**DIRECTIONS TO START**  The National Trust Pencarrow Head car park is situated on the Polruan to Polperro coast road, about one mile east of Polruan.

**WALK DIRECTIONS**

Return to the car park entrance and turn left. At the T-junction turn right (signed to Polruan). About 200 yards along the road, climb over a stile on the left marked for the National Trust property of Pencarrow Head. Walk straight up the field, keeping to the left-hand side. Pass through a gate in the left corner and then turn immediate right, over a stile and walk downhill. There are lovely views here across Lantic Bay with Pencarrow Head just to the left. It is now a case of following the coastpath, crossing stiles and gates as encountered.

From adjacent to the National Trust sign for Black Bottle Rock can be seen the red and white striped daymark on Gribbin Head (explored in walk 45). Pass through a series of gates and a stile before eventually nearing Polruan and passing a viewpoint bench in a small walled enclosure. Follow the path through a gate and along a short track to reach the road.

Turn left and walk along the road, passing a school. Immediately opposite a children's playground (a toilet block is nearby), bear right to follow a descending concrete path with a handrail. At the bottom of the path, bear right on a road. On reaching the road that descends to the quay, turn left and walk downhill (there are a number of places to eat here if required).

Once you have finished at the quay, retrace your steps uphill for a few yards and take the first road left (East Street - marked with a footpath sign to 'The Hills'). At the first set of steps, bear right up further steps, walking alongside a metal handrail between cottages. Where the handrail finishes, walk on for a few yards and then bear left, using concrete steps to eventually follow a narrow track. The track passes viewpoint benches, one of which is at a fork in the track. Keep to the higher (i.e. right) one, following an

obvious route through the woods. Use a partly made track for a few yards before bearing left on a further woodland track signed for Pont and Bodinnick.

The path eventually climbs to reach a three finger waymark post. Continue ahead signed to Pont and Bodinnick (Lanteglos Church will be reached by another route) and pass over a stile. An obvious track gradually descends, Pont Pill creek below left. Pass down steps and over a stile before continuing down steps to reach a path. Divert left for a few moments to visit the head of Pont Pill; note the lime kiln and a sign on the house dated 1894 giving the dues required for discharging items such as grain and timber.

Return back up the same path, walking past the footpath on which you arrived, to take stone steps to a road. Turn left for a few yards and then bear right through a gate marked as a footpath to the church. Walk uphill to pass through a gate to reach Lanteglos Church. Walk up the path in front of the church and through a gate, turning left and walking downhill, Churchtown Farm on the right. Keeping to the road, walk uphill and follow the road right, eventually returning to the car park on the left from where you started.

DISTANCE
4
MILES

TIME
2.5
HOURS

MAP REF.
ORDNANCE SURVEY LANDRANGER 200
149 514

WALK
MODERATE
GRADE

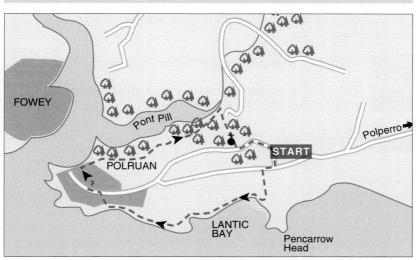

*Polperro. MDN*

# POLPERRO AND TALLAND

*Even if you have never been to Polperro, it is likely that you will have seen pictures of the village, because neither calendar nor book of photographs on Cornwall is complete without it. The attraction for photographers, and visitors in their thousands, are the narrow streets of whitewashed cottages leading to a well preserved and still active fishing harbour. In other words, a classic example of a Cornish fishing village. Although tourism is now the main focus of the area, Polperro originally developed as a fishing and smuggling centre in the thirteenth century. In its heyday four to five hundred years later, the catching and processing of enormous shoals of pilchards employed people for miles around. Nowadays, some fishing remains with boat trips providing for an alternative source of income.*

**REFRESHMENTS & TOILETS**   In Polperro (start point) and at Talland (mid point).

**DIRECTIONS TO START**   The A387 into Polperro ends at the main village car park (and start point for this walk) at Crumplehorn.

## WALK DIRECTIONS

Walk out of the car park and past Crumplehorn Mill on the left with its restored watermill. Head down the road into the main part of the village. Do not follow the road right at the bottom but continue ahead, near to the Post Office, slightly uphill to take a further right signed to the harbour and smuggling museum. Ignore the right turn across a bridge next to the House on Props and continue along the left side of the harbour. Pass a house covered in shells and the Heritage Museum on the right and proceed out past the harbour, following an ascending tarmac path.

At a split in the path next to a National Trust sign for The Warren, keep left. The tarmac path gradually gives way to an unmade track between hedges. Continue ahead on the coastpath, enjoying the sea views. At a fork in the path, bear right (signed Talland) to eventually reach a stone cross with lovely views towards Talland. Behind Talland Church can be seen a daymark, one of two that measures the nautical mile for mariners. Continue on the coastpath, passing a National Trust sign for Talland Cliff. Follow a tarmac driveway right until it bears left. Here, bear right, signed for the coastpath and after steps, walk steeply downhill to Talland Bay. If you wish to visit the interesting church at Talland, follow the road from the beach before returning back to this point.

Retrace your earlier steps back from Talland Beach by turning left along the road in front of a house and following the coastpath uphill. Where the coastpath bears left (the route on which you arrived), continue straight ahead on a tarmac lane, walking steeply uphill. Pass the driveway of a large house on the left and continue to climb, the road eventually levelling off to reach a road (ignore a stile on the left, signed to the coastpath). Walk straight ahead, passing houses and a school. The road eventually narrows before reaching a T-junction surrounded by trees. Bear left, walking steeply downhill, passing houses to reach Polperro once again. Keep right and now retrace your earlier route from the village towards Crumplehorn and your car.

**WALK**

# 47

**DISTANCE**

# 3

**MILES**

**TIME**

# 1.5

**HOURS**

**MAP REF.**

ORDNANCE SURVEY LANDRANGER 201

# 205 515

WALK **TOUGH** GRADE

*Talland Beach. MDN*

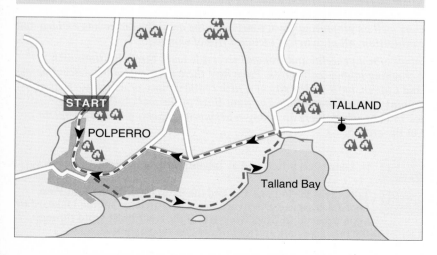

*Banjo Pier, Looe. MDN*

# LOOE, KILMINORTH WOODS AND TALLAND

*Divided into East and West Looe by a tidal river estuary, Looe is a popular holiday resort as well as an active fishing port and centre for shark angling. The town's attractions include a good beach, local history museum and a number of shops and restaurants. Although busy with visitors throughout the summer, the town retains a certain charm; its brightly coloured fishing boats a reminder of the importance of fishing as well as tourism to the town. If you want to find out more about this area, the South East Cornwall Discovery Centre, near the car park at the start of this walk, is well worth a visit. As well as promoting green tourism in the area, the centre has a video and photographic exhibition, all of which is included free of charge.*

*This route provides for a peaceful and tranquil riverside walk through Kilminorth Woods before climbing inland to Tencreek. From here there is an enjoyable descent across fields to Talland Church, built on the site of a fifth century place of worship, itself an excellent viewpoint across Talland Bay. The final third of the walk follows the coastpath back to Looe where there are many refreshment opportunities to complete your day out in the area.*

| | |
|---|---|
| **REFRESHMENTS & TOILETS** | In Looe (start point) and at Talland Beach (midpoint). |
| **DIRECTIONS TO START** | Take the A387 to Looe and use the main town car park in West Looe (also signed Discovery Centre). If arriving on the Liskeard to Looe regional railway, walk across the river bridge and through the main car park in front of the Discovery Centre. |

## WALK DIRECTIONS

Walk to the far end of the car park (i.e. furthest away from West Looe town). Follow the signs indicating a riverside walk to Watergate, walking with the West Looe River below to your right. At Watergate, emerge onto a tarmac lane and bear left, following the lane uphill away from attractive cottages. Continue up a fairly steep hill (ignore the bridleway signed on the left), walking past a holiday cottage complex on the right and also ignoring a public footpath sign on the left shortly afterwards. Stay with the lane, gradually climbing, the views becoming more far reaching as you continue, before eventually reaching the main road to Looe (A387).

Cross the road with care and follow a lane ahead marked for Waylands Farm. When the lane starts to bear to the left, cross a stile ahead and walk down the right hand side of a camping field. Near its end, pass over a stile on the right before following a well defined path diagonally (right) across the field. At the end of the field (close to where electricity cables pass overhead), pass through a gate opening. Follow the direction of the waymark arrow (i.e.

bearing right), staying close to the top edge of the field (ahead can be seen the top of the church at Talland).

Walk down the side of the right hand boundary - ahead is one of two landmarks measuring the nautical mile for mariners - keep to the right of this. Pass over a stile at the bottom and go down steps to reach a tarmac lane. Turn right and follow the lane to Talland Church (this is worth an exploration and there is also a nice viewpoint over the bay from the churchyard). Proceed downhill from the church to reach Talland Beach.

At the bottom of the lane, adjacent to a cottage, bear left signed for the coastpath. It is now a case of following the coastpath back to Looe, passing through the National Trust property of Hendersick en-route. The coastpath here is fairly level and undemanding; St George's Island soon comes into view. The final field path proceeds through Hannafore (toilets here) before continuing into West Looe via steps on the right that provides access to a quayside walk. Go underneath the main river bridge and pass shops before reaching the start of the main car park once again.

WALK
48

DISTANCE
7
MILES

TIME
3.5
HOURS

MAP REF.
ORDNANCE
SURVEY
LANDRANGER
201
252
538

WALK TOUGH GRADE

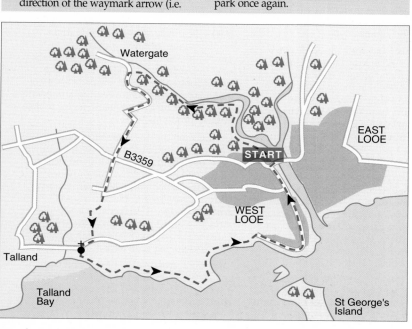

# LISKEARD TO LOOE VIA HERODSFOOT

*This is the longest walk in the book and the only route that relies on a train to complete the circular course. The return back to Liskeard from Looe is via the Looe Valley Regional Railway, completed in 1860 to transport copper ore and granite but now providing an eight mile (twenty minutes) scenic trip through the steep-sided valley of the East Looe River.*

*This walk relies on the Looe Valley Line to return to the start point. Please ensure train availability at Looe/Liskeard stations or by calling the national rail help-line on 0345 484950.*

**REFRESHMENTS & TOILETS** — In Liskeard (start point) and Looe (end point).

**DIRECTIONS TO START** — The walk starts from Liskeard Park and Ride Railway Station.

## WALK DIRECTIONS

Turn right out of the car park and walk up the hill, past the Railway Station. Turn left along the main road (B3254), walking across the bridge to reach a point where the road starts to bear left. Here, bear right on a single track road (signed Lamellion). Follow the road downhill, passing through Lamellion and then uphill away from the hamlet, gradually climbing to a road junction with a stone cross.

Cross the road and walk ahead, following a narrow lane. Where the lane bears right, turn left, walking along a track. At its end, turn right and follow the road for Scawns. Shortly after a large building on the left (Scawns Mill), bear left to take a narrow lane. At a fork in the lane, keep right and continue ahead until reaching a stile on the left (next to a gate) with a yellow waymark.

Cross the stile and turn right, keeping to the bottom edge of the field. A further stile leads to a path through light woodland, a stream below right. After a further stile, follow the obvious path ahead. Eventually pass through a gate and cross a stile just to the left of a barn. Bear right to follow a tarmac lane downhill before reaching a road at the village of Herodsfoot.

Turn right, crossing a bridge and follow the road signed for Lanreath, Pelynt and Looe. After a short distance, turn left (now signed only for Pelynt). The country lane now follows the route of the valley. Immediately after crossing a small stream, bear left to take a wide track that proceeds through woodland. At the end of the track, turn left and follow a tarmac road downhill. Do not cross the road bridge at the bottom, instead keeping right to follow a broad track marked as a public bridleway.

The track continues for some distance before reaching a clearing with a number of tracks. Bear left, crossing a small stone bridge, a lane continuing ahead before gradually descending to reach a path fork next to a small stream. Here, follow the public footpath sign left, crossing a stream and adjacent stile before bearing immediate right, following the waymark arrow, to take a track through a field.

Continue on the obvious route ahead, passing through bushes before emerging to cross open field again and a small stream. At the end of the field, a stile provides access to a woodland path again, the river below right. Cross a stile and a small wooden bridge. A further stile leads to an attractive broad path through the woods. Cross a further stile next to a large gate before emerging onto a road.

Turn right, crossing the bridge and walking uphill. Stay with the road until a junction where you should bear left signed for Kilminorth and Watergate. Stay with the lane until reaching the attractive cottages at

Watergate. Now bear left (public footpath sign) following a path that leads to Kilminorth Woods. Follow signs for the Riverside Walk to Looe, marked as a mile and a third in length.

The woodland walk continues with the West Looe River below left; a post with red/blue rings and a white arrow marks a discretionary higher path that can be used if desired.

After a pleasant woodland walk, the route reaches a generally level tarmac path that runs parallel with the West Looe River back towards Looe. Follow the path between the car park and the river and proceed towards the town. Cross the main river bridge and then bear left, walking up the road to find the railway station for your return journey to Liskeard.

WALK
49

DISTANCE
10
MILES

TIME
5
HOURS

MAP REF.
ORDNANCE
SURVEY
LANDRANGER
201
248
637

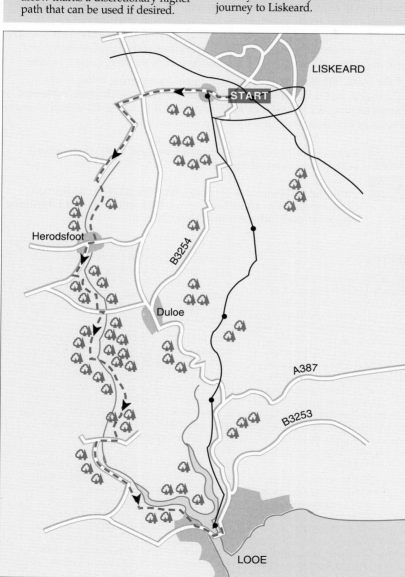

LISKEARD

START

Herodsfoot

B3254

Duloe

A387

B3253

LOOE

*Warning: Parts of this route can be muddy.*

# MAKER CHURCH AND CAWSAND BAY

*This walk is located on the far south eastern peninsula of Cornwall, overlooking Cawsand Bay and the approach to Plymouth Sound. It is an area that many visitors to Cornwall tend to overlook, especially since the growth in importance of the A30 holiday route, rather than the A38 Exeter-Plymouth road by which Cornwall was traditionally reached. The peninsula offers good opportunities for circular walks as well as the outstanding Mount Edgcumbe Country Park, reached at the end of the walk. This 850 acre facility includes 5 historic formal gardens and an historic house (admission charge and open during main holiday season only) with Edgcumbe family paintings and furniture.*

*Near the end of the walk, the route passes through the old smuggling villages of Kingsand and Cawsand. In truth, it is difficult to separate these settlements although until the nineteenth century, Kingsand was in Devon and Cawsand in Cornwall. A house with the old boundary line indicated on a wall is passed en-route.*

**REFRESHMENTS & TOILETS**

Pubs at Millbrook and Kingsand/Cawsand (both encountered within the course of the walk).

**DIRECTIONS TO START**

From the A374 towards Torpoint, take the B3247 to Millbrook. From here, follow signs for Cremyl. Park in the Mount Edgcumbe upper car park, adjacent to Maker Church.

## WALK DIRECTIONS

Walk back out of the car park, the way you arrived, and reach a public footpath sign on the right (signed for Empacombe) - this is a short distance from Maker Church on the left. Turn right on this path and walk down to pass through a gate and reach the road. Cross the road to take the path opposite, following a woodland path that descends to reach a broad woodland track. As indicated by the waymark, cross ahead, descending. The path bears left and then right, just inside the tree line from an open field. After a short distance, bear left through a kissing gate and walk down the field. A path descends, gradually bearing left and passing through a kissing gate to reach a road.

Do not take the public footpath opposite, instead turn left and follow the road for just under a mile. The road proceeds alongside the tidal creek of Millbrook Lake. At the end of the creek, take a road on the left (Higher Anderton Road) and carry on ahead through a residential area. The road gradually climbs before descending past Maker Lane on the left. At Millbrook, bear left at the junction

towards the Devon and Cornwall pub and then follow the road left signed to Torpoint and Cawsand. Reach a T-junction (B3247) and bear right for a few yards before crossing the road left to go over a stile with a footpath sign.

Bear left uphill, passing through a gap in the boundary at the top and then bear left on a track. Emerge onto an obvious grassy path that proceeds uphill, bearing slightly right. Pass through a gate in the top corner and an adjacent stile to walk on a half-right bearing across a field. Go over a stile to the right of a gate and cross the next field on a similar bearing. Pass over a stile to reach a tarmac lane.

Turn right and follow the road as it bears left shortly afterwards, walking uphill. Pass a public footpath sign on the left and follow the road as it bears right near a property. Shortly after passing a detached house on the right, find a public footpath sharp left. Take this grassy track, between hedges, adjacent to Wiggle Farmhouse. The track bears right from the farmhouse before bearing left near a wall and gate. Pass into a field adjacent to a concrete bunker.

Take the obvious path that crosses the field diagonally ahead and go through a kissing gate in the bottom corner. Follow a hedged track downhill. Proceed onto a driveway track to reach a road. Cross the road and take a kissing gate opposite. Now walk directly across the field, Plymouth Breakwater coming into view. Cross a stile next to a metal gate. Ignore the kissing gate on the left and use a grassy track that descends through a kissing gate to reach a road.

Cross the road to take St Andrews Street (signed as a restricted zone). This descends past cottages to reach a one-way street next to the Smugglers Inn. Turn left, walking uphill. Follow the road through Cawsand and shortly after passing a bakery, note the old Devon and Cornwall boundary sign on a house on the right. Walk on before turning right in front of the post office. Continue along The Cleave until reaching the Wreckers Restaurant. Here, take a narrow lane on the left (just before a small beach area), signed for the coastpath. Walk up between cottages to pass the Rising Sun pub on the left.

At the T-junction shortly afterwards, bear right to take the second turn on

the right (signed for Mount Edgcumbe Country Park). Pass through a gate and follow the obvious path (ahead can be seen a large property, this is Picklecombe Fort). Proceed ahead, leaving the grassy area behind to pass through bracken and scrub, eventually entering an area of woodland. Continue on the broad track, emerging from the trees again, before descending to pass through a gate and reach a road.

Turn right and then bear left (signed Mount Edgcumbe Country Park Coastpath) through a kissing gate. A narrow track climbs ahead, running roughly parallel with the road below right. Proceed past a bench and through a gate, following a woodland track ahead. At a path fork, keep to the higher, waymarked path, shortly afterwards reaching a track coming down from the left. Turn sharp left to take this track, climbing gradually to pass through a gate and out of the woodland.

Stay with the wide track that leads ahead, gradually bearing right. The stony track passes around the top of a small valley, passing a bench with far-reaching sea views. Continue, climbing towards trees and Maker Church. Proceed through a gate to reach your car.

WALK
50

DISTANCE
5
MILES

TIME
3
HOURS

MAP REF.
ORDNANCE SURVEY LANDRANGER 201
447
522

WALK MODERATE GRADE

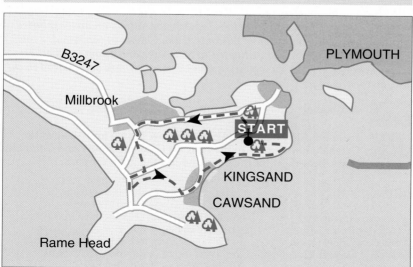

# COTEHELE AND THE DANESCOMBE VALLEY

*Cotehele, situated in the heart of the fertile farming country surrounding the River Tamar, has been in the care of the National Trust since 1947. The 1300 acre estate, previously owned by the Edgcumbe family for six centuries, includes a medieval house, gardens and woodland as well as an historic quay, visited by Queen Victoria in 1846. The estate was the first in the country to be handed over to the Trust in lieu of death duties and is now preserved for visitors to explore and enjoy.*

*This gentle walk starts from Cotehele Quay, adjacent to the River Tamar, using broad, well-made woodland tracks before exploring the Danescombe Valley, an area exploited in previous centuries for copper and arsenic. En-route is the Chapel in the Wood, a one room chapel overlooking the Tamar and dedicated to St George and Thomas a Becket. Nearby is the far-reaching Calstock Viewpoint, an impressive outlook over a bend in the Tamar towards Calstock Viaduct.*

**REFRESHMENTS & TOILETS** At Cotehele Quay (start point).

**DIRECTIONS TO START** From the A390 near Gunnislake, follow brown tourist signs for Cotehele until a split in the road for Cotehele House and Cotehele Quay. Bear right for the quay and use the main car park.

## WALK DIRECTIONS

Walk back towards the entrance to the car park and join a woodland path (signed Danescombe) adjacent to an information board (near to Cotehele Gallery). Do not take the stepped path on the left (which leads to the medieval house - admission charged), instead walk along a broad level track through woods. Stay with the main track, gradually gaining height to reach the Chapel in the Wood - a plaque inside the chapel details the escape of Richard Edgcumbe of Cotehele from Sir Henry Trenowth of

Bodrugan in the late fifteenth century - the chapel is said to date from this time.

Stay with the lower path that leads away from the chapel (the upper path leads through a gate into Cotehele Gardens), remaining on a broad woodland track that bears sharp right to reach the Calstock Viewpoint. Continue from the viewpoint (again ignoring a gated path that leads into the estate gardens), the woodland path soon descending.

The track descends to reach a T-junction in a broad track. Bear left and shortly afterwards walk past the ruins of Danescombe Sawmill. The track gradually climbs, following the course of a stream before passing to the right of two National Trust holiday cottages. Follow the track over the stream and after a short distance, cross the stream left over a bridge (next to the converted engine house of the Cotehele Consols Mine). Take the footpath to the right, walking near to the stream.

Pass around a small pond adjacent to a filled-in mine shaft, surrounded by a stone wall. An obvious path leads through the woods to reach a path fork at the bottom of steps. Bear left up the steps to reach a track climbing right to left before you. Turn left and walk uphill through the woods. Continue on, ignoring side paths, before climbing to join a broad woodland track. Carry on, walking through an area of coniferous woodland. Stay with the main path, ignoring side routes. The path eventually narrows a little and reaches a fork, the wider track on the right leading to a gate. Ignore this, instead bear left on the narrower path that leads downhill through the trees to reach the broad track used earlier.

Walk ahead, bearing right if you wish to visit Cotehele House and gardens (the house is open April to October only - admission charged). Otherwise, keep left, retracing your steps past Calstock Viewpoint and the Chapel in the Wood, following the broad track used earlier, back to the car park.

WALK
51

DISTANCE
2
MILES

TIME
1
HOUR

MAP REF.
ORDNANCE
SURVEY
LANDRANGER
201
424
682

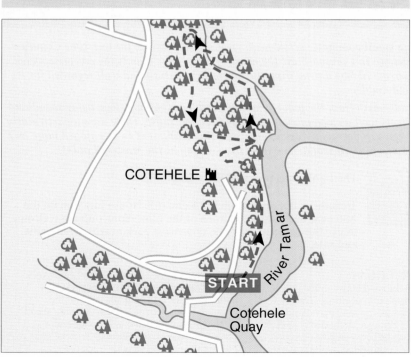

COTEHELE

River Tamar

START

Cotehele Quay

*Eliot Arms, Tregadillet. MDN*

# TREGADILLET AND THE KENSEY VALLEY

*Tregadillet is a small commuter settlement, west of Launceston, the one-time County town and 'gateway to Cornwall'. At the heart of the village stands the creeper covered Eliot Arms pub, a building dating from the fourteenth century and well regarded for its atmosphere and ambience.*

*This walk heads north from the pub to explore the quiet Kensey Valley, using woodland and field paths as well as a country lane, little used by traffic. There are no particularly outstanding views or deeply historical sights on this walk; it is to be enjoyed more as a rural, get away from it all walk, benefiting from an Inn at the start/end point!*

**REFRESHMENTS & TOILETS**  The Eliot Arms pub is at the start point.

**DIRECTIONS TO START**  Tregadillet is signed from the Kennards House junction on the A30 near Launceston. Patrons of the Eliot Arms pub are welcome to use the adjacent car park, otherwise park nearby where able and safe.

## WALK DIRECTIONS

Walk down the road between the pub and its car park, crossing a cul-de-sac (Dennis Gardens). Follow the road ahead and turn right shortly before a Methodist chapel. A stony track leads between houses to find and cross a stile. As indicated by the waymark arrow, bear right to reach a metal gate. Again as indicated by a waymark post, bear left after the gate, and walk ahead with the boundary immediate left. Cross a stile ahead, following a path between a hedge and a fence. At its end, pass through a metal gate and walk ahead on a wide track between hedges. Pass through a metal gate.

Shortly before emerging onto a tarmac lane in front of houses, turn left through a further gate (signed as a public footpath). Walk downhill on the right-hand side, passing through a gate on the right next to a waymark post. Follow a grassy track leading towards trees. Keep to the main path, using a further gate and walk ahead. Eventually cross a stile to reach an open field again. Bear half-right downhill to find and cross a stile. Proceed on a track that descends adjacent to a fence inside the woods. Eventually pass through a gate and walk diagonally down the field to cross a stile and reach a tarmac lane.

Turn left and follow the quiet country lane ahead (ignore the left signed to Tregadillet) for a little short of a mile. Reach a detached farmhouse on the left and as indicated by a waymark, bear left through gates into the farmyard. Bear left for a few yards on a concrete track before passing through a gate to enter a field. A muddy track leads uphill through a further gate. Continue uphill, skirting

to the side of an area of woods. Pass through a gate in the top left corner and walk on, keeping to the left. As you near the top of the field, bear right to pass through a metal gate, top right. Walk ahead along the top of the field, passing through a gate to cross a field in the same direction.

Bear left (waymarked) to reach a gate in the top right corner. Walk ahead on a wide track between hedges, eventually emerging onto a concrete driveway near a farm. Proceed ahead to reach a junction of tracks, marked with a large, four-sided waymark. Turn left on a tarmac lane, passing a bungalow on the left. Where the lane bears right, continue ahead through a metal gate, crossing a small field to a stile in the hedgerow. After the stile, bear half-left to use a further stile. Walk half-left again to cross a stile and enter woodland. Proceed over the footbridge, following a track on the other side that leads to a road. Turn right to reach the Methodist chapel again. Turn right in front of the chapel, retracing the earlier route back to the start point.

DISTANCE
3.5
MILES

TIME
2
HOURS

MAP REF.
ORDNANCE SURVEY LANDRANGER 201
297
837

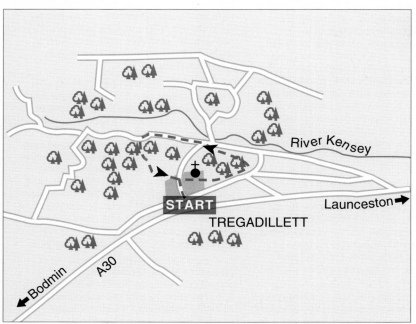

Warning: Parts of this route can be muddy.

# CAMELFORD, WATERGATE AND ADVENT CHURCH

*Camelford is a small market town on the north western edge of Bodmin Moor. The town takes its name from the Cornish "cam" meaning "crooked" and refers of course to the River Camel, astride which the town is located. The older parts of Camelford are essentially Victorian and Georgian in architecture although there has certainly been a market town here since the thirteenth century; the town prospering from its position on the main communication route in north Cornwall. Situated opposite the start point car park for this walk is the North Cornwall Museum and Gallery. This houses an exhibition on life in the area over the last couple of centuries as well as the local Tourist Info Centre.*

*This five mile circular route uses field paths and quiet country lanes to reach an ancient monolith before proceeding to the tiny church at Advent. From here, woodland and riverside paths are utilised to return to Camelford where there are a number of restaurants, pubs and tea-rooms.*

**REFRESHMENTS & TOILETS**
In Camelford (toilets in Enfield Park).

**DIRECTIONS TO START**
Follow signs for the Tourist Info. Centre from the A39 in Camelford. Use a car park opposite the North Cornwall Museum.

## WALK DIRECTIONS

Leave the car park and walk downhill. Turn left and proceed down the main road into the centre of Camelford. After crossing the River Camel, take the first right (College Road). Follow the road uphill. Continue until reaching a point where the road starts to descend right. Cross a slate stile on the left (marked with a public footpath sign) and walk keeping close to the right hand hedge before bearing slightly left to reach and cross a further slate stile. Walk downhill and cross a footbridge before passing through a gate and following a waymark arrow pointing uphill. Pass to the right of trees at the top and proceed along a lane, accessed via a gate. Continue on the lane until reaching a tarmac road.

Ignore a waymark left and turn right. After approx. 100 yards, turn left across a slate stile into a field. Head downhill aiming for the middle of the field boundary at the bottom. Cross a fairly well hidden footbridge over a stream and walk adjacent to the boundary fence on the right. Cross a stile and pass a house before using a metal gate to reach a tarmac road.

Turn left and follow the lane uphill, ignoring the first left turn before taking the second left, a road opposite a small row of cottages. Walk

uphill, eventually passing an isolated stone house and barn on the left. Approximately 250 yards after the stone house find a public footpath sign on the right. Pass over the stile and continue ahead, staying adjacent to the right hand field boundary. Continue past the Long Stone, a 10 foot high monolith placed here at least 2,000 years ago, before bearing slightly left and crossing over a stile in the wire fence ahead.

As indicated by the waymark, turn left and continue straight ahead to reach a stone stile between two gates. Cross the stile and walk ahead adjacent to the right hand boundary. At the end of the wall/fence, do not pass right through a gate opening but instead keep walking in the same direction as before, to the left of a wire fence. Shortly before reaching conifer trees, cross a stile right and take a half left bearing ahead. Cross two stiles in the far left corner of the field and walk with the fence and stream on your left. Pass along a small stone causeway and over a stile next to a gate to reach the tarmac road at Watergate.

Turn right and follow the road, walking gradually uphill and continuing for a considerable distance. Shortly before reaching a road junction, locate a public footpath sign and stile on the right. Cross the stile and proceed ahead following a path that gradually curves towards the right hand hedge to find and pass over a stile. Now turn left and walk downhill adjacent to the left-hand side field boundary. After a further stile, continue downhill, gradually veering away from the hedge on the left to pass over a stile located to the right of a farm building. Cross a small field and two stiles. Now bear right across the field and use a stile and gate to enter Advent churchyard.

After exploring the church, do not leave by the main gate but instead bear right in front of the church to find a metal gate and wooden stile. Head down the field on the right-hand side to find a stile adjacent to a stone footbridge across a small stream. After the footbridge, bear slightly left before walking ahead with a large pond on the left and a building ahead on the right. A stile provides access to a tarmac road.

Turn right. Shortly after a holiday cottage complex, look for a public footpath sign on the left. Cross the stile and walk downhill, keeping to the left.

After a short distance, descend right and pass through a small copse before crossing the river via a footbridge. Bear half right heading towards woods. Follow the obvious path up through the woods before crossing a large slate stile. Now bear half right across the field before using a stile next to a gate gap and proceeding ahead on the right hand side. Pass through a gate to reach a road.

Walk downhill (ignore the public footpath sign on the left) to reach a river bridge. Take the public footpath on the left and follow the riverside path, passing through several kissing gates, the last one being at the end of the water works on the left. Cross a field to reach a footbridge on the right that leads to the path being on the right of the river for a while before a stile and footbridge takes the path back once again. Follow the now tarmac path back along the river to the main road in Camelford. Turn left, retracing your steps uphill before turning right into Clease Road and walking back to your car.

WALK
53

DISTANCE
5
MILES

TIME
2.5
HOURS

MAP REF.
ORDNANCE SURVEY LANDRANGER 200
105
836

WALK MODERATE GRADE

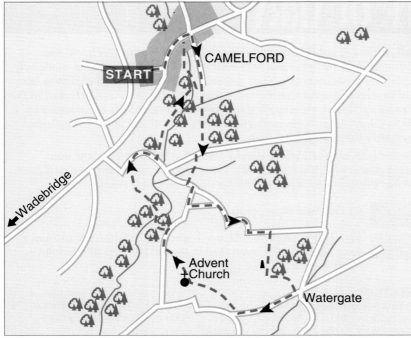

START
CAMELFORD
Wadebridge
Advent
+Church
Watergate

*Delabole Slate Quarry. MDN*

# A WALK NEAR DELABOLE SLATE QUARRY

*This short walk, although not the most exciting route contained in this book, has however been included for its opportunity to visit and view the largest man-made hole in Britain, viz Delabole Slate Quarry. Slate is known to have been extracted from here for about 700 years; certainly the Cornish word* **poll,** *meaning 'pit', was attached to the name Deli as early as 1284. A viewing platform provides an excellent opportunity to survey the 500 feet deep, 1.5 mile circumference quarry; the village pub, the Bettle and Chisel is named after the quarrymens' tools.*

*Nearby are the ten turbines of Delabole Wind Farm, established in 1991 and now producing enough power for 3,000 households. The adjacent visitor centre (open Easter until October) has displays and models of all forms of renewable energy.*

**REFRESHMENTS & TOILETS**    In Delabole (start point).

**DIRECTIONS TO START**    Delabole is on the B3314, north west of Camelford. Start from a long lay-by on the main road in the village, opposite St John's Church.

## WALK DIRECTIONS

Assuming you have parked opposite the church (toilet block nearby), start to walk along the main road with the church on the right. Cross the main road and pass the Bettle and Chisel Inn and a school. Recross the road again and shortly after a garage, turn left down a tarmac lane (opposite

Treligga Downs Road). Walk past the entrance to a churchyard on the left to reach the bottom of the lane.

Turn left in front of a house, following a track from which you can see the turbines of nearby Delabole Wind Farm. The track bears around to the right, passing garages, before bearing right at a road and passing cottages. Bear right to walk up the road into the quarry complex and then bear left through a car parking area to find the quarry viewing platform (behind the time office).

To continue the walk, return to the entrance of the quarry and turn right, heading towards the fire station tower. Bear left along a wide track just before the fire station. The track passes to the rear of houses before reaching a kissing gate on the left next to three large vertical pieces of slate. Pass through this kissing gate and then bear right to walk in front of houses. Now follow a fenced grassy track to the side of a large bungalow. Cross a slate stile and a field, keeping to the left-hand side. Pass over a further stile and then cross a series of small fields via stiles.

In the final field, pass below farm buildings and then cross a stile in the top left corner. At a lane, turn left and walk uphill to reach the main road (B3314).

Cross the road with care to take the road opposite (signed Trebarwith Strand). Pass Home Farm on the right and walk past the last property on the left (with high walls). Shortly afterwards, find a stile on the left marked with a footpath sign (near a telegraph pole). The stile provides access to a broad grassy track. Ignore a footpath that leads up steps in the hedge on the left and follow the track as it bears left then right. Continue for approx. two thirds of a mile, crossing a stile en-route.

After a stile, the way ahead is via an unmade track. Shortly after cottages on the left, turn left through a small galvanised gate to use a slate path that runs alongside a fence. Pass through a gate at the end of the path and walk straight ahead along a residential road to reach the main road once again. Turn left and walk back through the village to return to your car.

WALK
54

DISTANCE
3
MILES

TIME
1.5
HOURS

MAP REF.
ORDNANCE
SURVEY
LANDRANGER
200
071
841

WALK EASY GRADE

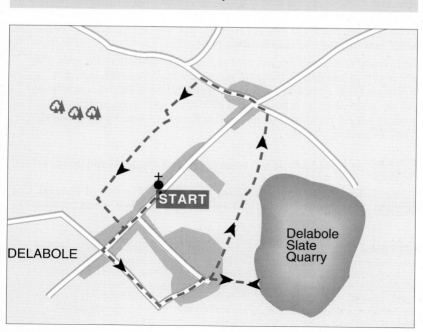

DELABOLE

START

Delabole
Slate
Quarry

*Trebarwith Strand. MDN*

# TREBARWITH STRAND AND TINTAGEL

*Although Tintagel is well known for its Arthurian connections, the debate about whether the area was home to such a king continues. A recent discovery of a slate, believed to date from the sixth century and referring to an 'Arthur' has added to the controversy. Whatever the truth, the English Heritage maintained ruins of the castle are certainly dramatically located and well worth a visit.*

*Much less controversial is the well documented exploitation of slate in the area. The coastpath route in the second half of the walk passes the well-known Lanterdan Quarry, an 80 foot pinnacle of rock at its centre denoting slate of inferior quality and therefore left by the quarrymen. It is amazing to think that one of the principal transportation methods for the slate was by boat; tall cranes lowering the mineral down the cliffside to waiting vessels.*

**REFRESHMENTS & TOILETS** — At Trebarwith Strand (start point) and Tintagel (mid point).

**DIRECTIONS TO START** — Trebarwith Strand is signed from the B3263 south of Tintagel. Use the large council car park on the right next to a grassy picnic area.

## WALK DIRECTIONS

Standing in the council car park with your back to the road on which you arrived, leave the far right corner of the car park. Head for the top right corner of the picnic area, walking gently uphill. Continue on a footpath signed for Treknow, reached after a stile. The footpath gradually climbs, passing over two stiles and up steps. As indicated by a waymark arrow, bear slightly left towards a gate in front of houses. Turn right along the road and walk ahead before turning right in front of a building with shutters (Briar Cottage).

At the road, turn left and follow it through the village of Treknow. Stay on the road, ignoring footpaths on both sides, to reach a T-junction. Turn left and at the bend, proceed on a lane on the left (signed for Youth Hostel). At the end of the lane next to Trevillick Farm, ignore the coastpath signs on the left and ahead but take a half-right towards a stone cottage (a further path is signed on the right over a stile - ignore this also).

After the cottage, proceed to a metal gate and adjacent stile. Cross the stile and small field ahead. After a stile in the left corner, walk with the hedge to your left, crossing a further stile, again keeping to the left. Pass a paddock and stable and over a stile next to a gate. Follow the track ahead and at a tarmac lane, bear right signed to the village. Follow the lane up into Tintagel.

At the main road, turn left. Shortly after a hotel on the left, bear left down a track signed to Tintagel Castle. If you wish to visit the castle, continue to the bottom, otherwise, cross left over the first footbridge encountered and follow a path that leads up the hillside. Cross a stile next to a gate to enter the

National Trust property of Glebe Cliff. At a path fork, keep left and follow the path ahead towards the church. Follow the path up beside a wall on the approach to the church, to reach a parking area and information board.

Take a narrow path to the left of the information board (heading towards the coast). Bear left at a wider track and then shortly afterwards look for a wider track on the right (the dramatically sited Youth Hostel below right). Bear left along the Hostel driveway for a few yards before taking a cliffside path on the right. Pass around Penhallic Point on a permitted path, enjoying stunning cliff landscapes that stretch back towards Trebarwith Strand. After a stile, follow the coastpath right. Pass over a slate stile into the National Trust property of Bagalow. A further slate stile is encountered before passing the 80 foot high pinnacle in the now defunct Lanterdan Slate Quarry.

Follow the obvious coastpath ahead. As it descends towards Trebarwith, ignore the footpath on the left and proceed down to the road. Turn left and walk up the road back to the car park.

DISTANCE
3.5
MILES

TIME
2
HOURS

MAP REF.
ORDNANCE
SURVEY
LANDRANGER
200
053
865

WALK MODERATE GRADE

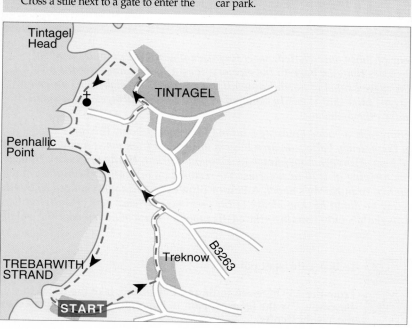

Tintagel Head

TINTAGEL

Penhallic Point

TREBARWITH STRAND

Treknow

B3263

START

*Minster Church, Boscastle. MDN*

# BOSCASTLE AND MINSTER CHURCH

*Boscastle is one of those once visited, never forgotten places that provides a visual stimulus that comes flooding back to the memory, long after you have left the area. Situated on the rugged coast of north Cornwall, the village was established around a notoriously jagged inlet that is easily explored - whitewashed cottages and a small breakwater add to the ambience.*

*This walk explores the wooded landscape, inland from the harbour. The route commences in the Valency Valley, an area largely unchanged from when a young Thomas Hardy walked here. Although now known as a famous author, Hardy originally trained as an architect, arriving in 1870 to supervise the restoration of nearby St Juliot's Church. The area is referred to in Hardy's novel, **A Pair of Blue Eyes**, the name changed to Castle Boterel, reflecting no doubt his knowledge of the previous existence here of Bottreaux Castle; the stronghold's only remains - the castle mound - is encountered near the end of the walk.*

**REFRESHMENTS & TOILETS**   In Boscastle (start point).

**DIRECTIONS TO START**   From the A39 between Bude and Camelford, take the B3263 to Boscastle. Use the large car park in the centre of the village next to the Visitor Centre.

## WALK DIRECTIONS

Walk to the far end of the car park (i.e. furthest from Visitor Centre) and pass a National Trust sign to enter Valency Valley. Walk alongside the river before following the hedge left to pass through a kissing gate in the top corner. An obvious path leads ahead up the valley. After a gate, the footpath enters woodland. Walk with the river on your right and past a crossing formed with stone posts. Pass through a kissing gate and continue through the woods until eventually reaching a wooden footbridge on the right (waymarked to Minster Church).

Cross the footbridge to take a footpath through Peter's Wood, gradually climbing up the side of the valley. Reach a waymark post at a path fork and bear right. Pass through a kissing gate to visit Minster Church.

Proceed up steps and bear right around the church before taking a tarmac path away from the church. At the road, turn right and walk on past a road on the left (next to a cottage marked Trecarne Gate). Follow the road as it bears right, downhill. Where the road starts to bear left, leave the road right over a stile. From here can be St Sampsons

Church and a white building on the right which was the old coastguard lookout station on Willapark Headland.

Proceed downhill, slightly to the left of the direction of the church to pass over a stile. Here, do not cross the stream but continue along the bottom of the field to use a kissing gate next to a footbridge. Again, do not cross, staying on the right of the stream and passing a cottage. Walk on the driveway away from the cottage and through a gate. At a fork in the driveway, keep left, passing properties to reach a tarmac road.

Turn right - this is the old main road of Boscastle - and walk downhill. Pass the Methodist Church on the right to reach a point where the road starts to bear left (there is a war memorial here also). Take a small tarmac path on the right to reach an area with picnic tables which has tremendous views - this was the site of Bottreaux Castle although little remains other than the castle mound.

Return to the road and turn right, walking downhill. At the bottom, take the opportunity to divert left and walk down the river to the harbour area before returning to your car - the free admission Visitor Centre is also well worth a visit.

WALK
56

DISTANCE
3
MILES

TIME
1.5
HOURS

MAP REF.
ORDNANCE SURVEY LANDRANGER 190
101
914

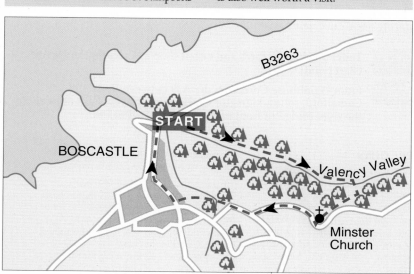

# CRACKINGTON HAVEN AND ST GENNYS CHURCH

*Crackington Haven, on the north coast between Boscastle and Bude, is an increasingly popular destination with visitors, a combination no doubt of interesting seascapes, good walking and a couple of refreshment opportunities adjacent to the beach! However, the area has always been popular with geologists; as you will see on this walk, there are many parts where the layered rock strata have been bent and crumpled to provide intriguing patterns in the cliffside.*

*The walk heads inland initially on a public footpath romantically called the Lovers Walk. After exploring the attractive church at St Gennys, the route follows the coastpath out onto Castle Point, so called because there is evidence of an Iron Age hillfort here, dating back 2,000 years.*

**REFRESHMENTS & TOILETS**
Toilet block, pub, cafés and beach shop at Crackington Haven (start point).

**DIRECTIONS TO START**
From Wainhouse Corner on the A39 between Bude and Camelford, follow signs for Crackington Haven. Park adjacent to the river bridge in front of the Coombe Barton Inn.

## WALK DIRECTIONS

Turn right out of the car park and follow the road as it leads behind the Coombe Barton Inn. Head uphill, passing houses and a parking area signed on the right. Find a public footpath on the right (Lovers Walk), shortly before a detached house. Take this footpath, a narrow track proceeding ahead, passing through a kissing gate to follow a woodland track. The track continues along the side of the valley before eventually passing over a stile to reach a narrow lane.

Turn left and walk uphill to reach a T-junction on the main Crackington road. Walk straight ahead and follow the road that climbs away on the other side. At a T-junction (with far-reaching rural views), turn left. Follow the road towards St Gennys Church. Ignore a sign for the coastpath on the left and proceed ahead to find a coastpath sign on the right, adjacent to a small parking area for the church. Although you will return to this point shortly, take a moment to walk ahead to visit the church - there is a particularly peaceful spot overlooking the coast at the far end of the churchyard. Now return to the coastpath sign near the parking area, descending steps and then bearing right from the large detached property. Walk down the driveway, a yellow waymark arrow indicates the path descends steps and through a gate on the right.

Follow a field path, with trees on the left, to walk through a gate in the far right corner. At the unmade track, bear left, following the track downhill. At the entrance to a further property, turn right to follow a tarmac track downhill leading to a grassy path over a stile/gate. Walk ahead, keeping the field boundary to your immediate left. Bear left with the boundary but do not take a path that is soon visible descending left. Instead, follow the edge of the field all the way around the far side. Shortly before bearing right towards a field boundary, take a grassy path that heads left and then almost immediately right, descending into scrub and light woodland.

Cross a footbridge and follow the obvious path up the other side. Cross a stile and turn left before then bearing right to follow the edge of an open field. In the corner, turn left next to a large waymark post and follow the top edge of the field straight ahead. Stay with the right-hand field boundary to reach the coastpath.

Turn left (on a clear day, the satellite dishes near Duckpool can be seen on the right), and follow the coastpath along the top of high cliffs. The coastpath descends a little, bearing left before crossing two adjacent stiles. Follow a grassy path ahead, soon crossing a further stile and following an obvious path out towards a pyramid shaped headland. At a National Trust sign for Cleave, carry on straight ahead, ignoring the inland path on the left. Continue until the end of the headland to find a track, leading downhill on the left, with steps in places.

Cross the stile and footbridge at the bottom and take the obvious path that zigzags up the other side. Pass through a kissing gate and take the coastpath right, following the boundary fence and going through a kissing gate (the headland of Cambeak can now be seen). The coastpath proceeds out towards the end of Pencannow Point before reaching a waymark indicating the coastpath now bears left towards Crackington Haven. Take this route, gradually descending to reach the road. Turn right and walk back to your car.

WALK
57

DISTANCE
3.5
MILES

TIME
2
HOURS

MAP REF.
ORDNANCE SURVEY LANDRANGER 190
144
968

WALK TOUGH GRADE

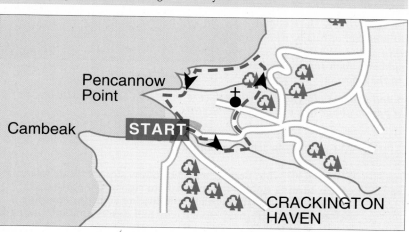

Pencannow Point

Cambeak

START

CRACKINGTON HAVEN

*Maer Cliff, Bude. MDN*

# CROOKLETS BEACH AND MAER CLIFF

The coastline of North Cornwall offers much for the walker and the area north of Bude is no exception. The route starts at the northernmost of the resort's two main beaches, Crooklets, and passes through the National Trust maintained landholding of Maer Cliff. This grassy plateau provides a relatively short walk to Northcott Mouth, also in the care of the Trust. The tranquil and almost isolated feel of this beach contrasts starkly with the more commercial and built upon surfing beaches of Bude, just to the south.

*Near Crooklets Beach, Bude. MDN*

This is a short and undemanding walk, although care should be taken, as always, on the coastpath that passes above low but treacherous cliffs.

**REFRESHMENTS & TOILETS**

At Crooklets Beach (start point).

**DIRECTIONS TO START**

Follow A3073 into Bude from A39. Follow signs to Bude town centre, turning right at the roundabout signed Car Parks and Beaches. Continue through town following signs for Poughill, before bearing left (near Somerfield) and descending into car park next to the beach.

## WALK DIRECTIONS

Walk from the car park towards the sea and bear right, passing Bude Surf Life Saving Club. Pass up steps to take a route in front of chalets that leads to an unmade road. Turn left and pass through a kissing gate to enter the National Trust property of Maer Cliff.

Proceed ahead across the grassy down. The coastpath crosses a stile, ahead can be seen the satellite dishes of the tracking station south of Morwenstow. Continue ahead, the coastpath gradually nearing a large white detached property on the approach to Northcott Mouth. Bear to the right of this property and head for two adjacent gates in the right-hand corner. Walk down the unmade track ahead, passing a parking area on the right to reach a road.

Turn right and follow the road, enjoying the far-reaching rural views.

Bear right with the road and pass a couple of properties on the right. Here, turn right (just before a thatched property) on a tarmac lane indicated as a bridleway. Walk past the entrance of Bude Holiday Park to reach a point where the road bears right. Turn left to take a wide track signed as a public bridleway. Stay on the track, between hedges, until eventually reaching a main road.

Turn right, following the road through a residential area. Cross Trevella Road and Ocean View Road and walk on passing the somewhat ornate Flexbury Park Methodist Church. Bear right into Flexbury Avenue and as an alternative to walking along the road, cross the road left to take a public footpath indicated along the edge of the golf course. Follow the path, parallel with the road before returning to the road, turning left and walking back to your car.

WALK
**58**

DISTANCE
**3**
MILES

TIME
**1.5**
HOURS

MAP REF.
ORDNANCE
SURVEY
LANDRANGER
190
**205
072**

WALK
**EASY**
GRADE

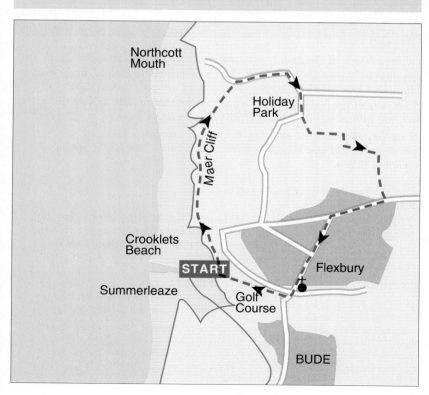

Northcott
Mouth

Holiday
Park

Maer Cliff

Crooklets
Beach

**START**

Summerleaze

Golf
Course

Flexbury

**BUDE**

# DUCKPOOL AND COOMBE WOODS

*The shale and shingle beach at Duckpool, situated in the isolated countryside south of Morwenstow, provides the start point for this short and enjoyable walk. Like several other parts of the coast here (and an amazing 40% of all Cornwall's coastline), Duckpool is in the care of the National Trust, ensuring the tranquillity and public access remains; a small toilet block has also thoughtfully been built.*

*After an initial section of quiet road walking, the route passes into Forestry Commission woodland of Coombe Woods before completing the circular route by returning to Duckpool Beach.*

**REFRESHMENTS & TOILETS** — Toilets at Duckpool (start point).

**DIRECTIONS TO START** — Leave the A39 half a mile south of Kilkhampton, following signs for Stibb. Pass through the village and down through a wooded valley. Turn left after a narrow road bridge and park near the beach.

## WALK DIRECTIONS

Walk back up the road from which you arrived and turn right over the road bridge. Follow the road uphill, climbing quite steeply up the wooded valley. At the sharp right bend, continue uphill, climbing away from the woodland to reach the National Trust owned property of Stowe Barton Farm. Continue to the end of the high wall next to the farm before bearing left through a gate, marked as a public footpath.

Bear right on a grassy path to reach a farm track. Turn right and immediately after a house on the left, bear right through a kissing gate. Turn immediately left to walk straight ahead, following a grassy path that gradually descends. Proceed into the woods via a stile, the track gradually bearing left and descending. Reach a parking area and bear right across the stream.

After a metal gate, follow the broad track as it bears left, walking downhill. The track bears left over a concrete bridge. At a track junction reached shortly afterwards, bear left, a broad level track now continuing ahead, a stream below left. At the end of the track, continue on a narrower and shadier path that proceeds in the same direction as before.

Join a tarmac road next to thatched properties at Coombe. Pass over a footbridge next to a ford and walk ahead. At a road, turn left and walk downhill for a few yards before bearing right (signed Duckpool) on

the road used earlier. Follow the road down the valley and back to your car.

*Coombe Woods. MDN*

WALK
**59**

DISTANCE
**3**
MILES

TIME
**1.5**
HOURS

MAP REF.
ORDNANCE
SURVEY
LANDRANGER
190
**202**
**117**

WALK
**MODERATE**
GRADE

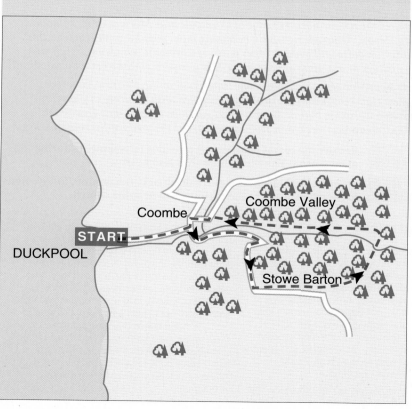

*Marsland Mouth. MDN*

# MORWENSTOW AND MARSLAND MOUTH

*This walk explores the remote northern edge of Cornwall near Morwenstow, adjacent to the border with Devon. Although rightfully becoming more popular with walkers, this area has an isolation quite unlike most other parts of Cornwall. Windswept cliffs and relatively few visitors at any time of year, make this a superb place to get way from it all.*

*The walk starts from Morwenstow Church, one time haunt of the eccentric Victorian clergyman, Robert Hawker. He was particularly concerned with ensuring shipwrecked sailors were given a Christian burial; the graveyard contains several such graves; the figurehead of the* **Caledonia***, wrecked in 1842, a reminder of the perils of the coastline here.*

**REFRESHMENTS & TOILETS** — Rectory tea-rooms (start point) provides refreshments during the main season. The Bush Inn pub is also nearby.

**DIRECTIONS TO START** — From the A39 just over 2 miles north of Kilkhampton, follow signs to Morwenstow. Use the parking area near the church.

## WALK DIRECTIONS

Cross the road from the parking area and walk through the lychgate or adjacent large slate stile (noting the white figurehead of the shipwrecked Caledonia ahead). Turn immediate right and follow a small gravel path downhill. Bear right to pass over a stile adjacent to the vicarage. Pass to the right of the vicarage (private property) and proceed on a track down into light woodland. Ignore a permissive path on the left and walk downhill to cross a footbridge.

Follow the path steeply up the other side and walk out from the trees to follow the right-hand field boundary. Pass through a gate and walk ahead to cross a ladder stile in the top field boundary (ignore a path signed on the right through the farm). Now turn right and walk along the top of the field and through a gate in the right corner. Bear left. Shortly before reaching a concrete driveway (the farm now below right), bear left and pass through the right-hand one of two adjacent gates. Walk up the field keeping to the left side. Cross a stile and walk ahead, bearing right after a stone barn. Go through a gate and follow a track between hedges to reach a tarmac lane.

Turn left and after a short distance (i.e. before

a farm), take a gate on the right indicated as an alternative path to the farmyard. Walk ahead before crossing to a gate in the left-hand boundary. Now turn right, walking between high hedges. The track bears left before passing through a large gate and continuing adjacent to the right-hand side. After passing through a gate, cross the field half left, onto a path leading to a slate stile. Continue in the same direction (or around the left boundary if the field has just been sown) to find a stile just before woods.

A partly stepped path leads down through the trees before crossing a footbridge. Follow the muddy path up the other side. At the top, turn right as indicated by a waymark, walking towards a row of trees. Bear right after the trees and then immediate left to walk along the top edge of the field. A stile leads to a narrow lane. Turn left and proceed gradually uphill to pass Marsland Manor on the left. Where the road bends right, turn left down a lane marked as a dead-end (also signed Marsland Mouth). Pass through a gate and descend with the lane before bearing left at a path fork next to a house. At a further path fork, keep right and follow the track as it descends (passing a memorial stone). The stream in the valley below right

marks the border between Devon and Cornwall. The track descends towards Marsland Mouth. Do not however proceed all the way down to the sea, but instead, follow the coastpath that bears uphill on the left. After a fairly long climb, cross a stile to reach a seat at the top of Marsland Cliff.

Follow the coastpath down into Litter Mouth, using steps before crossing a footbridge and climbing steeply up the other side. The route now crosses five stiles before descending on a right bearing into Yeol Mouth. Cross a footbridge and stile before ascending up the other side. Follow the coastal waymarks, passing along Henna Cliff. After crossing a stile, the satellite dishes near Coombe come into view. Walk ahead with Morwenstow Church now in view to the left. At a waymark post just before the descent into the valley in front of the church, turn left to follow a traceable path heading towards the vicarage. This path runs along the bottom of cultivated fields, gradually descending along the valley. Cross a stile and walk along the bottom of the field to reach a point used near the start of the walk. Turn right and retrace your earlier steps over the footbridge and back beside the vicarage. Cross the stile to re-enter the churchyard and walk back to your car.

WALK
60
DISTANCE
4.5
MILES
TIME
3
HOURS
MAP REF.
ORDNANCE SURVEY LANDRANGER 190
207
154

WALK TOUGH GRADE

*Warning: Parts of this route can be muddy.*

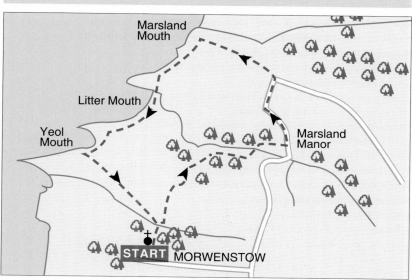

Marsland Mouth

Litter Mouth

Yeol Mouth

Marsland Manor

START   MORWENSTOW

# NOTES FOR WALKERS WITH CHILDREN

These notes are intended to provide further guidance to the suitability of individual routes for walkers with children. This section should be used in conjunction with the walk grading and distance in deciding the routes you would like to try first. Stout footwear is recommended at all times.

Although each of the walks in this book has been carefully researched and checked to ensure ease of use, particular care should be taken to follow the instructions closely when walking near cliffs. To determine which walks involve some form of cliff walking look for the symbol  ⚡  below. Always leave adequate daylight hours to complete your walk.

| | | |
|---|---|---|
| **1** | ⚡ | Coastpath and field walking with quiet country lanes also. |
| **2** | ⚡ | Narrow coastpath in parts, some uphill sections. |
| **3** | ⚡ | Some road walking in first half of route. |
| **4** | ⚡ | A little road walking. Overgrown in places. |
| **5** | ⚡ | Steep coastpath near start of walk. |
| **6** | | Some road walking involved and fairly muddy in places. |
| **7** | | Fairly overgrown paths and stiles in places. |
| **8** | ⚡ | Fairly strenuous coastpath walking in last half of route. |
| **9** | ⚡ | Level, well made paths and quiet country lanes. |
| **10** | ⚡ | Uses a fairly busy road for around 3/4 mile plus some overgrown inland paths. |
| **11** | ⚡ | Busy road for short distance in second half. Low level coastpath walking. |
| **12** | ⚡ | Although graded easy there is one short uphill section at mid point. |
| **13** | ⚡ | High and at times unstable cliffs, however, coastpath wide and firm underfoot. |
| **14** | ⚡ | Lots of coastpath walking with small uphill sections. |
| **15** | ⚡ | Though graded easy there is a fairly steep climb by lane near the start. |
| **16** | ⚡ | Strenuous walk using undulating coastpath. |
| **17** | | Uphill section away from Porthoustock. Some road walking. |
| **18** | | Some road walking that will be busy at times. |
| **19** | | Well made paths and quiet country lanes, suitable for children. |
| **20** | ⚡ | Low level coastpath and quiet country lane walk. |
| **21** | | Can be very windy, rocky underfoot in places. |
| **22** | ⚡ | Muddy in places with some close to the edge cliff walking. |
| **23** | | Low level woodland and country walk suitable for children. |
| **24** | ⚡ | Fairly long route with some cliff walking. |
| **25** | | Some road walking and uphill in places. |
| **26** | ⚡ | Rocky cliff terrain and country lane walking. |
| **27** | | Low level easy going, suitable for children. |
| **28** | ⚡ | Busy road crossed on two occasions. |
| **29** | ⚡ | Uphill section at mid point. |

| | | |
|---|---|---|
| 30 | ⚡ | Coastpath narrow and hard going at times. |
| 31 | ⚡ | Tough walk with uphill sections and some road walking. |
| 32 | ⚡ | Tough walk with uphill sections and some road walking. |
| 33 | ⚡ | The route passes close to the cliff edge in places. |
| 34 | | Some uphill sections. |
| 35 | | One overgrown section, can be busy with cyclists in first half. |
| 36 | ⚡ | Tough undulating coastpath for fit only. |
| 37 | | Steep if short climb by road between Port Gaverne and Port Isaac at end of walk. |
| 38 | | One short uphill section near mid point. Firm underfoot. |
| 39 | | Some climbing involved but firm underfoot and traffic free. |
| 40 | | Uphill section by road at beginning. Overgrown section near end. |
| 41 | | Long road section in middle (though generally quiet in terms of traffic). |
| 42 | | Largely urban or road walking. Uphill section at beginning. |
| 43 | | Road walking in second half. Short uphill section in middle. |
| 44 | | A couple of uphill sections and some country lane walking. |
| 45 | ⚡ | Long walk, undulating coastpath in places, some cliffs. |
| 46 | ⚡ | Coastpath walking close to edge in parts. Some uphill sections. |
| 47 | ⚡ | Short walk although comprising uphill sections, hence tough classification. |
| 48 | ⚡ | Long, steep country lane at mid point. Some low cliff walking. |
| 49 | | Long walk, uphill in parts with country lanes. |
| 50 | | Road walking in several parts, some uphill sections. |
| 51 | | Easy, level walking suitable for children. |
| 52 | | Some uphill walking plus country lane (generally quiet). |
| 53 | | Hard going in places, long uphill road section at mid point. |
| 54 | | Generally level walking, busy road crossed twice. |
| 55 | ⚡ | Dramatic coastpath walking above high cliffs. Tough in parts. |
| 56 | | One uphill section at midpoint (though gradual). Some road walking. |
| 57 | ⚡ | Hard coastpath sections in parts. Some road walking. |
| 58 | ⚡ | Low level cliffs and lane walking. Partly urban. |
| 59 | | Steep road section near beginning. |
| 60 | ⚡ | Hardgoing coastpath sections for fit only. |

# INDEX

*Monument, Carn Brea (walk 21). MDN*